# MY CHILD IS GAY

**Bryce McDougall** was born in 1967. He lived on the Hawkesbury River at Ebenezer for the first eleven years of his life. In the late 70s his family moved to Sydney where he remains. This is his first book; a second is underway. Information will be updated at www.responsibility.com.au as it nears completion.

# MY CHILD IS GAY

## How parents react when they hear the news

Edited by

## Bryce McDougall

ALLEN & UNWIN

First published in 1998
This edition published in 2006

Allen & Unwin
83 Alexander Street
Crows Nest NSW 2065
Australia
Phone:   (61 2) 8425 0100
Fax:      (61 2) 9906 2218
Email:    info@allenandunwin.com
Web:     www.allenandunwin.com

National Library of Australia
Cataloguing-in-Publication entry:

My child is gay : how parents react when they hear the news.
ISBN 978 1 74175 124 6.

ISBN 1 74175 124 1.

1. Children - Sexual behavior.  2. Gays - Family
relationships.  3. Parents of gays.
I. McDougall, Bryce, 1967- .

306.766

Set in 11/13 pt Bembo by DOCUPRO, Canberra
Printed in Australia by Southwood Press, (02) 9560 5100

10 9 8 7 6 5 4 3 2 1

*And a woman who held a babe against her bosom said, Speak to*
*us of Children.*
*And he said:*
*Your children are not your children.*
*They are the sons and daughters of Life's longing for itself.*
*They come through you but not from you,*
*And though they are with you yet they belong not to you.*

*You may give them your love but not your thoughts,*
*For they have their own thoughts.*
*You may house their bodies but not their souls,*
*For their souls dwell in the house of tomorrow, which you cannot*
*visit, not even in your dreams.*
*You may strive to be like them, but seek not to make them like*
*you.*
*For life goes not backward nor tarries with yesterday.*
*You are the bows from which your children as living arrows are*
*sent forth.*
*The archer sees the mark upon the path of the infinite, and He*
*bends you with His might that His arrows may go swift and far.*
*Let your bending in the Archer's hand be for gladness;*
*For even as He loves the arrow that flies, so He loves also the*
*bow that is stable.*

*The Prophet*—Kahil Gibran

# CONTENTS

# ACKNOWLEDGEMENTS

I would like to say a special thank you to the following people who helped me, had faith in me and supported the idea. Some have offered advice, some friendship, others support, and many all three. The biggest thank you must go to the parents who have contributed their stories. For your desire to help other parents by putting your feelings into words, I thank you. This book would not be a reality if it were not for you.

To all of the following people who I have at one time or another talked with about the concept and bounced ideas off— thank you. To the many others who I have not mentioned, especially my work colleagues, thank you too.

Andreas Lippa, Andy Murphy, Brian Roberts, Bruce Chapman, Bruce McKenzie, Bryan Davey, Chris Lucas, Coral-Lea Benzie, Darran Chadwick, David Bishop, David Britt, David Hely, David Rooney, Derek Williams, Donna Bridges, Dr Brett Wayne, Dr George Bearham, Dr Peter Pigott, Dr Ruby Banerjee, Dr Sandy Beveridge, Dr Wayne Sherson, Esme Devine, Fahren LeVeree, Frank Di Benedetto, Gary Sutton, Geoff Whytcross, Gerard Glover, Graeme Aitken, Graham Swann, Guy Mitchell, Hazel Cowen, Heidi Van Houten, Helen Smith, Hugh Greenough, Jan McDonald, Jane Larucci, Jason Sambrook, John Hahir, John Mallon, John McCrow, John Noble, Jonathan Saurine, Kim Fyfe, Lisa Jervis, Louisa Leary, Mark Kelly, Michael Kinsella, Michael McGlinchey, Murray Altham, Neil McCammon, Pamela Du Valle, Paul Anstee, Paul Paisio, Peter Booth, Phil Timmins, Ray Wines, Rob Rogan, Robyn Musker, Ross Foley, Russell Bullen, Sean Linkson, Shane O'Hare, Simon Darling, Stephen Mangos, Stephen

Yates, Steve Biddulph, Steev Cole, Steve Schmidt, Steven Godbee, Terry Stewart, Tina McDougall, Tony Madden, Warren Whalen, Wayne McDougall.

Extra special thanks to: Andy Palmer from Hodder, who gave me many helpful tips; Bryce Courtenay; Dr Ratna Banerjee, who read some original drafts; and Eric Oass, who told me to read a book called *After the Ball*, which motivated me to write this book.

Heather Horntvedt, who cofounded PFLAG, gave me a tremendous amount of assistance, as did John and Margaret Pugh. John Melvey, my partner of three years, has given me a wealth of feedback and inspiration. Many thanks to Margaret Sullivan—the book would have fallen over without you. Michael Jones listened to my often incessant discussions about this and that, and Myles Grindal helped me with some information about his generation— ha ha Myles. Phil Dows helped me enormously in the early stages, and Richard Lyle gave me excellent ideas and helpful contacts. I lived under Rob Small's roof for twelve months while working on this project—how you survived, I don't know. Sophie Cunningham, my publisher at Allen & Unwin, had the faith in the idea that has carried this book through to the bookshelves. And finally, special thanks to Tony Nuzzo, who for fifteen years has remained my best friend and supports me in everything I do.

## Copyright acknowledgements

I gratefully acknowledge the following material which has been reproduced in this book.

Quote on pp. 163–4 is from Ann Thompson Cook, *Issue Paper 2*, Respect all Youth project, INSITE, and Federation of Parents and Friends of Lesbians and Gays, Washington, DC, 1991. Reproduced with permission of the author.

Quote on pp. 165–6 is from Steve Biddulph, *Manhood: An Action Plan for Changing Men's Lives*, 2nd edition, Finch Publishing, 1995. Reproduced with permission of the author.

Quotes on pp. 168 and 169 are from Adam M. Tomison, 'Update on Child Sexual Abuse', Issues in Child Abuse Prevention, Australian Institute of Family Studies, No. 5, Summer 1995, pp. 2, 5. Reproduced with permission of the author.

Excerpt on pp. 178–84 is from Bryce Courtenay, *April Fool's Day*, Reed Books, Melbourne, 1995. Reproduced with permission of the author and publisher.

# INTRODUCTION

My *Child is Gay* is a compilation of letters written by parents who have a gay son or lesbian daughter. Fifty parents from Australia and New Zealand have written their stories in the hope that they can be of help to other families.

Some writers have chosen anonymity, thinking that this is the only way in which they can be open about their feelings. Other writers have felt it important that they identify themselves and their families as a show of solidarity with their child. With a candour that is often painful, but rarely without humour and compassion, each writer charts their journey towards an understanding and acceptance of their child's sexuality.

There is no 'perfect', or textbook response to the revelation that a son or daughter is gay or lesbian. Emotions can run wild and confused feelings such as anger and embarrassment can quickly surface. Parents may also feel guilty that their child has struggled alone, and can find themselves asking, What caused this? Where do I turn for help? What about grandchildren? What will people think? Can my child live a happy and fulfilled life?

The feelings and opinions of each parent are sometimes contradictory, but overall there is a common thread. Again and again in the letters, parents talk about the resources they have discovered that have helped them to dispel the myths surrounding homosexuality. It is of vital importance that parents speak with someone well informed, be they a professional counsellor, a Gayline counsellor, a member of PFLAG (Parents and Friends of Lesbians and Gays) or a friend. It is also useful to read widely on the subject and watch films and documentaries. Good books can be recommended by PFLAG or you can search the Amazon website (at www.amazon.com) under 'Parents of Gays'.

PFLAG is a group of dedicated parents and friends who volunteer their time to help other parents, and they also offer help and support to gay or lesbian people who are contemplating coming out to their families. PFLAG's motto is 'Keeping families together'. Amongst other services, they offer support and advice over the phone. They are happy to forward helpful literature, and they have regular meetings where parents can get together and discuss their experiences.

PFLAG Australia was founded in Perth in the mid-eighties and now has branches in just about all states. Contact numbers for PFLAG and a similar group in New Zealand are also listed in the 'Further Information' section.

I was overwhelmed by offers of encouragement and support while I worked on *My Child is Gay*. It was clear that a book of this nature was sorely needed, not only for families, but for gays and lesbians. Help was certainly not easy to find when, at the age of seventeen, I told my parents I was gay.

Just before the 'Further Information' section is an excerpt from Bryce Courtenay's book, *April Fool's Day*, which recounts one of the struggles his own family faced when his son, Damon, became HIV-positive through a blood transfusion. I wanted to include this extract because it shows how we can hurt each other so deeply through silence. *My Child is Gay* is a book that celebrates the importance of voice, and the ways in which speaking out can be at once intensely painful and liberating. Coming out may be the most confronting, difficult challenge a young adult will ever face. I hope that the honesty at work in these letters will make the road easier.

# LETTERS

*Written by John Pugh from Perth. Born in Collie in 1932, John trained as a radiographer at Princess Margaret Hospital and then worked at Fremantle Hospital for 34 years. John and his wife, Margaret, were married in 1955 and have two sons, both of whom have been with their partners since 1980. In 1989 they met June, who was a member of the US support group, PFLAG. Together they initiated the first meeting of PFLAG in Western Australia on 2 December 1989.*

On a warm autumn day in March 1980, something was about to happen that would change the whole course of our family's life, something we never dreamed could possibly happen to us.

Jeff, our son, had been a bit 'uptight' for some time, but when he went off one day and didn't come home all night, by next morning my wife, Margaret, and I were naturally a bit worried. By lunchtime we were really concerned, but on hearing his car come into the driveway, a great feeling of relief came over us.

After some time, we were puzzled that he had not come inside and I was about to go out and voice my concern on his overnight absence. Margaret, however, restrained me, in a mother's knowing way, and said that we should wait a little while longer.

'I've got something to tell you,' Jeff said, when he finally came inside, 'perhaps you had better sit down.'

We seated ourselves in our lounge, Margaret next to Jeff and myself nearby. Many thoughts raced through my mind in those next few moments: drugs, trouble with a girl (on reflection, this thought is now quite funny), a felony of some kind, money problems—what could be worrying him? It was obvious something had him deeply troubled.

Then, with that tiny phrase 'I'm gay', our world was turned upside down.

From that moment our lives started on a new course, which was to bring untold tears, secrecy, frustration, confusion and also intense annoyance with people and their attitudes. We would, however, eventually find many new friends and a great joy that we have only found in the gay community.

In the minutes that followed Jeff's disclosure, we asked all the questions that parents seem to ask, I guess.

'How do you know you're gay?'

'How long have you known?'

'Are you sure? Perhaps you may change your mind later on.'

'Have you told anyone else?'

'No.'

I remember saying, 'Isn't it wrong?'—something that I felt deeply sorry about afterwards. He gave us answers that we didn't particularly want to hear.

On that first day I guess we blundered around, somewhat stunned and not knowing what to do. Who could we talk to about homosexuality? Maybe we could find someone who would tell us it may only be a passing phase. Foolishly, I thought Jeff might change his mind when he found out what it was really all about.

Our elder son, Graeme, was out visiting his fiancée, Sue, at the time, so we rang him and asked him to come home because a family crisis had developed that we couldn't discuss over the phone. After arriving home and expressing his disbelief at the news, he suggested that we try to contact Gayline. So he and Margaret went across the road, to a public phone box, to be out of earshot, and rang Gayline.

The man on the phone only confirmed our worst fears. He said, 'If Jeff is 21 and has done a lot of soul-searching [as he said he had] and has come to the conclusion that he is gay, then to imagine him being able to live his life as heterosexual is quite impossible.' He said that we had to change our lives to accommodate the new person that had come into our midst.

Looking back, two things that the man on Gayline said proved to be very important to us at the time.

1. 'It is OK to be gay, you know.'
2. 'You, as parents, must be very special for Jeff to have come out to you first. Most gay people are afraid to do this because they fear their parents will react badly. Initially, they usually tell only siblings and close friends.'

I guess, at the time, this gave us a little lift. Many gay people that we have met over the years since have told us this. What they fear most about coming out is the adverse reaction of family members, particularly parents. Jeff said, years later, in a radio interview, that coming out to Mum and Dad was the hardest thing he had ever done.

At first we had many sleepless nights, wondering what to do. We realised that we knew so very little about homosexuality. We had never had the strong antagonism that lots of folk seem to have towards these 'other people', but, like many, we gave it little thought because it didn't concern us. In my ignorance I imagined that a 'good woman' was the answer for a gay man and likewise a 'good man' the answer for a lesbian woman. I certainly had a very long way to go.

So we began searching for information about homosexuality and commenced a long self-educating process. This gave us a much deeper understanding of homosexual people and their problems and changed many ideas and beliefs that we previously held, especially about sexuality in general. However, finding any positive reading matter in 1980 proved to be very difficult. Very little gay literature was readily available at that time. Besides, it's very hard to ask in libraries and bookshops for books about something that you are afraid to talk about. Nevertheless, in time we did become more bold, the fears gradually left us and our library of gay books grew steadily.

In the meantime, Graeme, in fear and concern, had to explain things to Sue. She was a close friend of Jeff, too, and although completely surprised, she took it in her stride. Jeff was her friend and whether he was straight or gay made no difference to her.

She went to the top in our estimation. Jeff was best man at Graeme and Sue's wedding and there has been a strong bond between them ever since. This bond was extended to Jeff's partner, Graham, when he joined the family. Now there are children, and uncles Jeff and Graham are a popular part of their lives too. I anticipate and hope that they will grow up free of any prejudice towards homosexual people.

Until this time, we thought of ourselves as a happy, fairly normal, middle-class, suburban family—maybe we were a bit smug and complacent. Margaret and I both worked full-time. We were both very involved with and held positions in the Uniting Church. Our social life revolved around the church. However, our boys had long since decided that the church had no interest for them and we accepted that.

Our own disillusionment with the church probably began when AIDS raised its ugly head. The church had to be seen as caring for people with AIDS, but it was very careful not to be seen as accepting homosexuality. We tried, for some time, to educate people by becoming involved in various groups. Some people understood, but mostly they just felt sorry that we had this 'dreadful problem', a gay son. As time went by we became interested and involved with the Universal Fellowship of Metropolitan Community Churches. The MCC was founded, in 1969, in the USA by the Reverend Troy Perry, who was rejected by his own church because he was gay. It is now a rapidly growing church, particularly in America but also throughout the world. In the MCC we found a love and acceptance that we had not felt before in any other church to which we had belonged.

For a time, Margaret and I were involved in the Social Justice Working Group of the Uniting Church, and amongst the group members we found some wonderful support. However, one of the members told us once that the Social Justice group was the most hated group of the Uniting Church and naturally we came to this conclusion ourselves too. I guess, in the end we realised that all that was to be gained from the church was sympathy, not acceptance and understanding. Sympathy alone was something we could do without. So after much painful deliberation, we eventually severed our connection with the Uniting Church and started to direct our energy towards places where we felt the real need existed, like PFLAG and MCC.

We still feel that although the churches may be talking about the acceptance of homosexuality, when it comes to voting to accept openly homosexual persons, they will eventually back away. We hope we are proved wrong.

When Michael Chamberlain was asked in an interview if he had lost his faith, he said, 'No! but I have lost the baggage that went with it.' After shedding some of our baggage, we now feel privileged that we have been allowed to share in the love, joy, friendship, sufferings and sadness of the gay community. Unfortunately, however, there are still tears, frustration and sometimes intense annoyance at the attitudes some people, particularly 'Christians', show towards the homosexual issue and the gay people we have grown to love.

For a year or two after Jeff came out, I searched deeply, trying to find a reason for him becoming gay. Was there something we, as parents, had done or hadn't done? Had we treated him badly or differently from his elder brother? Had there been some major crisis that could have caused a psychological upset? Jeff assured us that the answer to all these questions was, 'No!' Nothing we had done or should have done would have made any difference.

As I saw it, Jeff had a good and perfectly normal childhood. He gave his mother few problems being born. Somehow we knew it was going to be a boy—even the doctor said so—despite the lack of ultrasound in those days. I guess most parents do their learning on the firstborn, so he had the benefit of some experience on our part. Although different in nature from his brother, he was still very much a boy. He developed the usual boisterous nature that boys have, managing to get hurt on many occasions. He loved his teddy bear and soon developed an attraction for toy cars and things mechanical. Of course, toys needed to be tough to survive rough treatment but we thought he was overdoing things when he tested the strength of a Matchbox toy in a workshop vice.

Jeff was always generous by nature and his money box always had to be accessible. If it wasn't, it was soon made to be, so he was usually broke. However, none of our family ever went without a birthday or Christmas present, even if it meant borrowing money to buy one. His membership in Cub and Scouts led to him becoming a Pack Leader, but his interest in Scouting waned a few years after joining a senior Scouts group.

Jeff was never keen on sporting activity but probably compensated, to some extent, by doing very well academically, winning top-of-the-class awards in two subjects in his final year at high school and gaining his Bachelor of Business degree with distinction.

Like most siblings, Jeff and Graeme fought with each other most of their young lives, but almost overnight, when they were fourteen and sixteen years old, their fighting stopped. We've often wondered why. Since then they've been good friends. From primary school days, both boys had positive ideas on their careers. Accounting was Jeff's aim in life and motor mechanics that of his brother. Both achieved their ambitions and have continued in these careers.

In the early times, we knew very little about gay relationships, and were a little concerned at what Jeff might do to this end. However, he had his own ideas on finding a partner, and this was by advertising in one of the local newspapers. So, in this way, he met Graham.

After Graeme and Sue were married, Jeff stayed on living at home for a month or so and one day casually asked us if we would mind if he moved out into a flat of his own. Naturally, we said that would be OK, as long as he was happy doing that. 'Oh well,' he said, 'as long as you don't mind, I'll be going now.' Anticipating our reply, he had things packed and was ready to leave.

So, all of a sudden, our family was gone, leaving Margaret and me with the strange, empty feeling you get when they all finally leave. You're glad, in a way, to see them go but deeply sad that they are not there to care for any more. All the activities that a family generates suddenly stop and a strange quiet seems to descend. Now both boys had gone, our elder son Graeme with his new wife and Jeff to a new friend unknown to us.

We first met Graham some time later when Jeff persuaded him to come to dinner with us one evening. He said he came trembling with fear. Naturally, we were concerned that Jeff may have teamed up with someone we would dislike. However, we should have had enough trust in Jeff's judgement to know he wouldn't choose just anyone. We took an immediate liking to Graham and he grew steadily to be like one of our family.

Apart from Graham's mum, it would be a few years before we met two other parents. With them and a number of gay people and their families we formed a small support group, Uniting Friends. But where were all the other parents? Our small group eventually disbanded, but during the fight for homosexual law reform in Western Australia in 1989–90, we joined in the parliamentary debate with many gays and lesbians and some parents. From this campaign, together with our friend June, we gathered together the parents of lesbians and gays that we knew and on 2 December 1989 PFLAG was born in Western Australia. A year or two later, one of the group members, Heather, moved to Sydney and started a PFLAG group there. PFLAG is now spreading throughout Australia.

So our dream for many years at last became a reality. A support group for parents at our own time of need would have been so wonderful.

I still get angry at parents who cannot or will not accept their child's homosexuality. Maybe they can't understand, but many won't even try. I still don't fully understand, all these years later. I guess that I never will, because I'm heterosexual. However, there is no real reason for parents to refuse to accept a gay son or lesbian daughter. What many people give as excuses are purely selfish matters that will upset their own lives and relationships. Isn't the life of a son or daughter worth more than that? I believe that the love we profess to have for our children is truly tested when we first hear that little phrase, 'I'm gay', from one of them. How we behave then will reflect the true depth of that love we profess to have.

Margaret and I are so grateful that Jeff had the courage to tell us first about his homosexuality. In retrospect, however, we were so sorry that he carried the burden alone for all of his teenage years.

We are happy that he has found a soulmate in Graham and that they have worked hard at maintaining a lasting, loving relationship.

I like to think that Jeff knew we loved him a lot when he first came out, and that he knew we would accept him, as he was, no matter what. I like to think that he was right.

Most helpful books:
*My Son Eric*
*Beyond Acceptance*
*Coming Out: An Act of Love*
*But Lord They're Gay*
*Good News for Modern Gays*
*Ex Gays? There are None!*
*Is the Homosexual my Neighbor?*
*Living in Sin? A Bishop Rethinks Sexuality*
*The Church and the Homosexual*
*Yours with Pride: Letters to my Gay Son*
*Now That You Know*

*Written by Deirdre Monk from Tasmania. Deirdre is president of PFLAG's branch in Hobart and is a proud mother and community and volunteer worker. A self-professed 'bad violin player', Deidre is an avid music lover.*

I have known about our daughter's sexuality since 1990. She was then in her mid-twenties, and she was living in Western Australia. She is a master puppeteer and was working over there.

She announced that she was in love with another woman and was lesbian in a phone call one Friday evening. I can recall the time, day and date and what I was watching on TV. I never did see the finish of *The Prince and the Show Girl*.

The news came as a great shock to me and it took a long time for it to sink in. I woke my husband and tried to tell him, but he was not a lot of help. First reactions were, what will people say? I want my daughter to have children. I want grandchildren. Where have we gone wrong? Who is to blame? All of the usual reactions that you have heard before.

I handled it alone for a while; my husband was not keen to

discuss it. We both accepted the fact and kept in mind that she was still our lovely daughter and we would never turn our back on her.

My daughter and I wrote long, revealing letters for twelve months before we actually were reunited on a trip home for Christmas. She wanted to bring her partner of that time with her, but I had to refuse as we really could not handle it so early in the process of coming to terms with the whole thing.

The reunion was a happy one and we needed that time to get used to the idea that we had a lesbian daughter. We have since met her partner and have had them here to stay. Their relationship is now over and Heather has not formed another relationship. The biggest heartache I have is that she will grow old and lonely and perhaps not have someone to love and comfort her in her older years.

I think I was guilty of being homophobic in the past. I was ignorant about the subject and didn't want to know about it. But when it comes to your own family, it creates a very different situation.

I have come a long way in my understanding of homosexuality, but I still need a great deal of support and sometimes it's easy just to sit down and have a good cry. My husband has a long way to go before he reaches the stage that I am at, and finds it hard to discuss homosexuality with male friends and family members. Yet he is very understanding and loves our daughter very much.

Having formed the PFLAG support group has been a great leap forward for me and I can really feel just how it was for my daughter when she came out for the first time. Now I have been in print I feel I have come out to the wider community. Last week I wrote a letter to the *Mercury* dealing with the concerns we have as parents about the extension of prison terms for the criminal code, which includes homosexual acts between consenting adults. This would now bring a 25-year prison term should they be convicted. I have had nothing but favourable comments since it was printed and the support and love out in the community is very comforting.

Our daughter is very proud of the way we are coming to terms with her and the homosexual community. We have grown so much closer as the result of the journey of understanding, and will continue to fight for the dignity and human rights of the whole of the homosexual community in Tasmania and the mainland states of Australia.

Most helpful books:
*Parents Matter*
*Different Daughters*
*Invisible Families*

*Written by a mother of four—three girls and a boy—from Tasmania. Born into a large family with missionary parents, she is a retired teacher of small children. She wished to quote a pertinent passage from the Bible, Luke 6:37: Judge not and ye shall not be judged, condemn not and ye shall not be condemned.*

My daughter realised she was different from other girls when she was in her early teens. She was seventeen when she told me she was a lesbian. Feelings of dismay, sadness and even guilt swept over me. Where had we gone wrong? Had we failed to give her sufficient love and guidance? Could anything be done to help her? My family doctor seemed to think it was 'too late' once awakened. He said another woman could understand the desires and needs of another female. Her announcement was not a complete shock. I had wondered, because she always hated girls' clothing and was pretty much a tomboy. She was very attracted to me at an early age, when most girls absolutely adore their father.

The next few years were not easy for my daughter or me. She became friendly with a group of lesbians, some of whom were rather hard and bitter. She shared a house with some who didn't like us to visit. I suffered agonies as to whether I should accept her or take her to a psychiatrist or doctor. I know how much harder life can be for people who are 'different' . . . I hoped she might 'grow out of it'.

Having a strong Christian background was a stumbling block. Did the Bible really find it abhorrent to love someone of the same sex? This may be the point where I can help. I do not know how God feels about this matter. What I do know is that Jesus taught love. His message was, 'A new commandment I give unto you that you love one another, even as I have loved you.' (John 13:34)

As a modern, fairly well-educated person I believe that many people are homosexual naturally and therefore it is not a 'sin', even though doubts still linger in my mind. One important thing I try to remember is that we are not the judges. I know some truly Christian people who can forgive a daughter's adultery, but not a son's homosexuality. It is people like that whom I would wish to help.

Both my husband and I have been so fortunate to be accepted by our daughter's partner and friends. Even so, it has been hard for us as parents. How do we introduce our daughter's partner to our conservative friends? I hedged the question for years. 'This is her friend,' I used to say. A hurt daughter remonstrated with me. 'Mum, we are not friends, we are lovers.' With such difficulties, I am aware how much more of a struggle it has been for my daughter.

Even though I already knew and accepted two acquaintances who were homosexual, it has been a long and slow learning process for me. I knew something of the battle that my friends had endured in their lives. Is this the life my daughter is going to have?

To reiterate for the moral judges—it is not our place to judge. As a parent of a grown person it should be our pleasure and duty to love, encourage and enjoy a close relationship with our family.

*Heather Horntvedt lives in Sydney's Hills District. Born in the UK in 1943, Heather and her parents moved to Australia in 1958 and her mother returned to England in 1961. Alone in a strange country at seventeen, Heather worked three jobs to support herself. She credits this period in her life for giving her the inner strength to cope with the adversities life has offered. After her first marriage ended, Heather*

*remarried in 1981, and says, 'Doug is the most wonderful stepfather to my two sons. They both idolise him.'*

I'll never forget that fateful Friday Robbie told me he was gay. He had asked me to sit down as he had something to tell me. I remember thinking it wasn't going to be a happy event, because of the tone in his voice. He just said, 'I never wanted to hurt you, but I can't go on living two lives. I have to tell you I'm gay.' We didn't say anything afterwards. I was tired and in shock, I suppose. I'd just got home from work. Robbie started to get ready to go out for the evening as he usually did on Friday nights. I think I did what I normally would, a bit like a robot, but later that night when the realisation came to the fore, the guilt, the devastation, I sobbed and sobbed.

I lay in bed wondering where I had gone wrong as a parent. I'd tried so hard to be a loving and responsible parent, but I must have failed somehow. No, it wasn't that—God was punishing me because I'd desperately wanted a daughter. When my second son had been born I'd taken pink clothes to the hospital, because I was so sure I'd have a girl, and I felt resentful and disappointed because he wasn't. I remembered dressing Sean in the pink clothes to take him home and saying to this tiny baby, 'That will teach you for being a boy.' It seemed like only yesterday and I was ashamed for being so resentful. It didn't last long—I loved that little baby—but it was an awful thing to say at the time. I couldn't have any more children and I'd been waiting for Robbie to get married, to give me a granddaughter, and this was God's revenge. 'No, don't be silly,' I told myself, 'it's because I was an overprotective mother and I'd divorced his father. Oh why me, what have I really done? Maybe he'll change back, he's confused.' Still I sobbed, and I cried for months. He didn't change!

We hardly spoke during the ensuing week, and I tried to act as if nothing had happened, but Robbie seemed so much more relaxed than before. The next weekend he brought home a video for me to watch with him. It was about an American medical student coming out to his family and their struggle in coming to terms with his homosexuality. It was unreal—everything that mother said and felt and did was ME! I cried and cried and

y hand and pass me tissues
oving and gentle with me.

much he must have been
o he really was, that he was
nother was just like me until
invited her son's lover over
Robbie, 'Don't ever expect
ome. I never want to meet
dready in a relationship with
der than himself, and I never

loved him and would try to
I'd be able to meet his gay
and his words of reassurance
ways been gay, and he was
g to be hard for me to finally
day at a time, and Robbie
for me to read and watch,
hurt festered, and it took a
but slowly I began to accept
ned to pride.

en years ago now, and how
much as a person, and my
anymore. We don't realise
our children. Most of the
ind out our child is gay are
lives and then they change
s, and we have no right to
re want them to. I'm less
who they are, not what they
o treat people how I'd like
rs been a sensitive and kind
d if my straight son marries
on't matter, as long as they
precious granddaughter isn't
have an automatic right to
sons is that they are happy.
to ask to be accepted? Do
cause we are heterosexual?

There's so much hatred and
are continually called on to f
people. I now know the m
a beautiful feeling.

Having been blessed witl
world for me. I've met and
and talented people. I get so
know. It's a pleasure to be
my social life tends to be wi
thing for me is that most o
and acceptance from their
parents can alienate one of
especially because of their
months after Robbie told m
him. How could I? He's sti
a more loving and loyal pe

If I hadn't had Robbie
many things. I've fought for
a founding member of bot
South Wales PFLAG group
and kept families together.
public in a world that is so
person. I'm trying to educa
it be through a television in
schools and welfare workers
a proud parent under the
exhilarating feeling.

I never did meet my s
years to cross that hurdle.
and he died on 2 Decemb
PFLAG meeting in Pertl
became very fond of, and
relationships didn't last ve
replace Chris. It hurts to
never met the most impor
as a member of the Austra
I came upon Chris's quilt
was fortunate that there v
into his quilt. I knelt dow

Robbie would hug me and hold
and tell me it was OK. He was

Years later, I now realise h
hurting. I was crying because of
not what I wanted him to be. Tha
the end of the movie, but then sh
to spend Christmas. I pleaded with
me to allow your lover into my
him. PROMISE me now!' He was
a television producer, twelve years o
wanted to confront it.

He promised! I told him that I
understand, with his help, and slow
friends, but not his lover. The mov
helped me to understand he had
not going to change, but it was goi
accept. I pretended to take each
brought as much as he could home
and was so patient. Deep down my
long, long time before I understood,
it and eventually my acceptance tur

That fateful Friday is over thirt
it has changed my life. I've grown s
values have changed. I'm not selfish
as parents how selfish we are with
reasons we are devastated when we
selfish reasons. We've planned their
our plans, but it's their life, not ou
expect them to live it the way v
judgemental and I accept people for
are. Even though I've always tried
to be treated, and I think I've alwa
person, I'm a nicer person now. An
a girl that can't have children, it v
love each other and are happy. That
so important now. Why should we
grandchildren? All I want for both m

Why should a homosexual have
we have to ask to be accepted be

olence in the world. Homosexuals
ive. I've never met such forgiving
ing of unconditional love and it's

i gay son has opened a whole new
ecome friends with so many lovely
much warmth from people I hardly
art of the gay community and even
h the gay community. The only sad
f Robbie's friends do not have love
families. I cannot understand how
their children for any reason, but
exuality. Even in those first few
he was gay, I never stopped loving
the same son I've always had, and
on one would never find.

I'd probably never have done so
human rights in parliament and been
the Western Australian and New
s. I've helped educate other parents
Somehow I found the courage to go
prejudiced—strange, I was such a shy
e as many people as I can, whether
terview or giving a talk or lecture to
. I've marched in six Mardi Gras as
PFLAG banner, and it has been an

on's lover as it took me about two
Chris was the love of Robbie's life,
er 1989, ironically the date of our first
h. I met his second partner, whom I
I've met his only other partner. Both
ry long. I don't think they could ever
think I was so naive for so long and
tant person in Robbie's life. However,
lian and New Zealand Quilts Project,
by accident a couple of years ago. I
vere two photographs of Chris sewn
n at first and just sobbed, asking his

forgiveness, and then I looked into his eyes, such beautiful eyes. I could see why Robbie had loved him so. I feel close to Chris now, and feel that we are at peace with each other. Every year I have his name on my list that I read out at the candlelight rally. Each year my list gets longer with the names of Robbie's friends and people I have known and been fond of. One has such a mixture of feelings, and yet our mourning the loss of loved ones gives us a sense of togetherness as our grief is shared. I've witnessed a love of life and a love that will never die.

I don't know what the future holds for me, or how long I will have my Robbie, but if I could wave a wand over him and make him heterosexual, I wouldn't do it. If I changed anything, however small, even a hair on his head, he wouldn't be my Robbie, and I love my Robbie just the way he is. Nobody can take away what we've had together, my memories and the love that is so special. Robbie has enriched my life and I thank God every day for giving me such a precious and wonderful son.

Most helpful books:
    *Beyond Acceptance*
    *But Lord They're Gay*

*This mother from Adelaide is a writer. Her letter, written from the heart at a delicate time, reflects the strength of the emotions she then felt. Things are better for her now, much better. She says now, 'It is a stage and it will pass, but at the time when it is real, we all have to show our humanity.'*

My initial feelings of anger and guilt are still with me, despite it being two years since my daughter told me of her homosexuality. I have additional feelings, too, none of which will help any other parent in dealing with this problem, but they just might make them feel that they are not alone in this dreadful mourning.

There's the guilt because my beautiful daughter is flawed. Was it my fault? Did I love her so much that she learned a woman's love is the only worthy thing? Or did I err in teaching her that girls are as good as the boys they're forced to compete with? Should I have let her play the sports she showed talent for, water-polo and cricket? A good mother might have forced her to play with dolls, and sit at home with her knitting and sewing. Blame! It never ends, but love can when reality intrudes.

Anger. Yes, I understand anger, too. Why me? Why can't I hand down to my grandchildren the drawings she did at kindergarten and the sweet little stories she wrote at primary school? She took her sporting trophies with her when she left, and a good thing, too, because if I had a continual reminder of her lifestyle, I'd only have another reason to cry every day.

I can't cope and I doubt that I ever will. Life is meaningless—she taught me that. I wasted my time marrying and producing children. If I hadn't done either, I could have saved myself all this heartbreak. Given my time again, I doubt I'd have children, and I'd do my best never to love anyone more than myself. This, I think, is called bitterness.

Then there's honesty, the hardest of all. I might hate myself for it but I wish she had died instead. What a trivial existence it seems, the life of a gay person. A half-life, with no births or marriages, other than a hypocritical relationship formed in imitation of a procreational couple. Betrayal is all I can see, betrayal of me as a mother. She rejects my beliefs, my principles and my femininity. Why? Was there something so hateful about my love that all she wanted to do was scorn me until the end of my days?

It seems unfair, but I'm not allowed to have any emotion over this. If I do, I'm being manipulative. She won't change her mind, and she made this choice, but guess what? My unhappiness puts pressure on her. So I'm not allowed to be unhappy. A good mother, I'm told, would be thrilled that her daughter has found peace. Perhaps she has, but she's destroyed mine. Since I'm not allowed to feel any emotion, or express my honest thoughts, all I can do is stop loving her. As she has no other choice, neither do I.

Yes, love dies. I tell myself this every day in the hope that it will happen to me. I can't forgive her, I can't respect her and I certainly can't understand her. I don't want to love her any longer.

*Written by a mother in her early fifties from Brisbane. She is a wife, mother and director of home duties and has been told she is a bit of a stirrer. She married her high school sweetheart 33 years ago. They have two children and their daughter is married with two of her own. Their son came out to them three years ago.*

'I'm gay', are words, I think, most parents can never be prepared for.

Our son, Steven, had been home from overseas for only two days when he came out to us, his family. He had left two years earlier to see the world, and we had no idea of his sexual orientation. As far as we had been aware he was no different from his mates—a fairly serious young man striving for perfection in all he did, what I called a high achiever. He had many friends, male and female, the odd girlfriend, but spent a lot of time studying for his profession.

We had always worked at being a close and caring family involved in many activities including Scouts, sports, camping and family get-togethers, and our children had a Christian upbringing. I had encouraged them to always tell the truth—'Nothing is as bad if you tell the truth.' I regretted ever having said this for quite some time after Steven told us he was gay!

I have had a problem not blaming myself, wondering where I went wrong and what we should have done differently, and I cannot find answers to my questions.

We all seemed to withdraw into our shells and were at a loss as to how to help each other—for myself, I just seemed to cry a lot. The family did not want to acknowledge that Steven's 'gayness' would last. Our love for Steven never changed, but we certainly needed help in understanding our situation.

Fortunately, I found a very understanding Salvation Army counsellor who was able to explain that what we were experiencing was grief over the loss of our hopes and dreams for Steven's future—to marry and have a family of his own. Our daughter and son-in-law had only recently had our first grandchild and now we had to come to terms with the realisation that we would miss this from Steven—his sister would miss nieces or nephews, and Steven would miss having children of his own. It was very difficult for us all. Our counsellor recommended we read several books, and it showed me our family is not alone and we need to try and feel positive and hang in there, and that, as time passes, it will be easier for us to accept and understand what has happened.

What I wanted was to find another mum in my situation—I still miss this—someone who has survived all these feelings and is there to offer understanding and support when I feel down.

Another difficulty has been deciding who we should tell—elderly grandparents, relatives, friends, workmates? After giving it a lot of thought, I have told Steven's maternal grandmother, who has been very supportive to us, and some of our friends. We have had the odd hurtful comment, but in the main they have been supportive too.

Society has given us many hang-ups concerning homosexuals, portraying them to be promiscuous, weak and unmanly, and seeking too much publicity. This has led to much misunderstanding and I can't help but worry about Steven's future. Not only do parents need to understand their child's situation but society in general needs to be better educated.

This time has not been easy for any of us, but we love Steven and never want to lose him. We want him to have a happy life and we want everyone to accept him as he is.

Most helpful book:
*Coming Out to Parents*

*Written by Stella Marie Anderson, a mother from Perth. Stella Marie was born in England and moved to Australia in 1980. She has two children, Steven and Tamar, and ten years ago married her second husband, Bob. She believes that when a child comes out to a parent, they are placing their trust in them, saying, 'I love you, this is who I am, please still love me.' She says, 'Love them unconditionally, support them, get to know your child.'*

Little did I realise on that bright and sunny Sunday morning some four years ago as I contemplated a relaxing hour with my coffee and the paper, that I was about to embark on a journey, my mind borne on the wings of time, down the long and winding road of memory.

The peaceful air on which the music of Mozart's *Symphony No. 41 in C* was gently flowing was fractured by the shrill sound of the telephone. 'Hello, Mum,' Tamar's sweet voice trickled down the line. 'Guess what?' She began to relate how the previous evening she had met two schoolfriends whom she hadn't seen for a couple of years. 'I've something to tell you, they're gay.' She hesitated, then continued in a rush. 'I've something else to tell you, so am I.'

The words reverberated in my brain: 'So am I, so am I.' Tamar and her friends were drawn together by our all-knowing subconscious and bound together by an invisible and fragile thread.

I gazed at the sky outside. It was still blue, the birds were still singing to each other in the trees and my daughter was a lesbian.

I began to feel an overwhelming sense of pain for the lonely inner life she must have led before coming out to me, for how difficult the travel down the road of realisation must have been. I also remember asking the inevitable, 'Are you sure?' regretting the words as they tumbled out. What a question. You never ask if a person is sure they are heterosexual. I assured my dear girl that I loved her and always would and I was there for her at all times.

Later, as I sat with my now rapidly cooling coffee, my mind continued travelling down memory's path. The years sped by and rested with my favourite cousin, Terence. Dear, gentle, gay Terence, with his laughing, teasing ways. The tears began to flow, salt-water rivulets wending their way down my cheeks as my thoughts centred on the tragic memory of his murder, ten years previously in London, not, I hasten to add, because he was gay. The motive was one of pure avarice, the desire to possess what he owned. Terence gone, no more to see that boyish smile, no more, no more. The shadows of the past cast dark shades upon memory's long road, blotting out the sunshine.

Tamar and I spoke the day after in a long and deep conversation between hugs, and although close, we have grown closer still.

After a time I began to feel a sense of isolation, wishing I knew other parents who had been blessed with gay children so that we could share a common bond. I discovered PFLAG by chance, through a brief mention in the community newspaper. As I am by nature reserved and hesitant, Bob, my rock, took the first step in the journey by telephoning PFLAG.

The day of our first meeting arrived, and my heart pounded with nervousness and uncertainty. I need not have feared as a new doorway along the road of life opened and I became part of a new 'family'.

My life has been further enriched by the arrival into Tamar's life of Jenny, almost four years ago. I have gained another 'daughter', another silver thread in life's tapestry, and I treasure time spent with them. My mind begins to move along the present road and my heart aches for those who have to struggle to come to terms with their sexuality and who long for the love and acceptance of family and friends. A person's sexuality is part of who we are. I long for people to come to the realisation that 'closets are for clothes, not people'. We must not hide our gay sons and daughters away, but love them, support them, stand proudly at their side.

For the past two years I have taken part in the Gay Pride march to join other parents as we say we are proud of our gay children. Our lives move on, never stationary upon our journey, always learning a little more, weaving new threads. Dear Terence, ever close in thought, I love you.

> He knows no sadness
> he does but smile
> and walk in peace
> upon the silent earth,
> to leave a trace
> that he has passed
> this way
> and hope they will remember.

This is part of a poem I wrote about Terence.

I will always remember. Tamar and Jenny, my dear girls, ever close to my heart, I love you.

*Written by a 60-year-old mother from Melbourne. Her husband is a businessman and they have three sons and one daughter. Two sons are married and there are three grandchildren. She is a musician and has been involved with teaching music for many years. She is a practising Christian and plays the organ in the Anglican church she attends.*

I will never forget the day that my son invited me to lunch and told me that he was gay. I thought it was going to be one of our very happy occasions when after lunch we would play music together. He plays the flute and sings as well as playing the piano. I have accompanied him for years. He is a fine musician as well as being a fine, caring son and doctor specialising in cancer. He was about 30 at the time.

He thought I would have guessed, but it is one of those things which one puts in the back of the mind, hoping it is not true. My very much loved son had been in agony for a long time, knowing that he was different. He told me that he was eight when he first realised that he was not the same as most people. He wanted to bring it into the open, frightened that we would hear it from somebody else. I thought my heart would break. He had kept this from us for many years, not deliberately, but, I think, not knowing how to broach the subject. He talked for about an hour and then he said, 'You're going to feel differently about me now, aren't you? And so will the rest of the family.'

I immediately denied this. How could I stop loving this wonderful, wonderful son? If anything I love him more. He is different. He is special. He then asked me what I thought about it. I replied, 'I think you drew the short straw.'

'Yes Mum, I did.'

I would like to explain why I said this. There are so many of these lovely, charming, gentle gay young men. In many cases they are joked about, looked down upon and definitely discriminated against. My son loves children. He will never have any of his own. Someone asked me why didn't he just marry and have a family. He would never do that to a woman, not when he could not be totally committed. I think homosexuality is one of the saddest things in the world, but let's be clear about something—there are far worse things. Shouldn't we be thankful? His gayness is only one part of him. Unfortunately it is with him all the time. In fact I think some gay men needlessly wear their homosexuality like a cloak which they can't seem to take off, whereas from where I sit they are just like everybody else, going about working at their jobs and in many, many cases doing much good in the community. What does it really matter? Except for the aura of sadness which never goes away. Of course we know this is caused by the attitude of many people, but do you know, I think we are improving! Most of us are not going around looking for their 'differentness'.

Fortunately, or unfortunately, his father has so far not seen any point in one-to-one discussion on the matter as he feels that this would not achieve anything. I think that, like many men, he finds it difficult and so prefers to regard and treat it as a background issue. He is still very caring and shows his support in many ways. My other two sons and daughter have never wavered in their love and support. The younger generation seem to be easier in accommodating such issues. We read what analytical material we can get our hands on about the subject. If any disparaging remarks are made about homosexuality I have been known to get on my soapbox and tell people what I know, to give them a more realistic perspective. We all need to be educated, some more than others.

I would guess that my letter is no different from many others, but I thought I would write just the same.

*Written by Norma Schwind from Perth. Norma and her husband, Bob, have a son and a daughter. The Schwinds feel there is no room for prejudice in society and hope their involvement with PFLAG will help*

*other parents to accept and support their children. They are family-oriented*
*and believe that legislation and social acceptance amounts to little or*
*nothing if children are not accepted and loved by their own families.*

The fifteenth of October 1992. It was a Thursday and we had
been to do the grocery shopping. I went into the house first
while Bob unpacked the car.

'Mum and Dad . . .'

A long white envelope lay on the counter. It was in Matthew's handwriting and instinctively I felt a sense of foreboding.

'Mum and Dad . . . I'm gay . . . I can't bear to see your
faces as you read this . . . I can never live up to the expectations
you have of me as a son . . . I love you all very much; you are
an important part of my life . . .'

Once, twice, three times I scanned the lines, not wanting to
believe. I hurried out to Bob, who was still unpacking. 'Brace
yourself, there's something from Matthew that you have to read.'

When worlds turn upside down, or seem to, what do you
do? In the first five minutes we decided we needed help. The
family as a unit has always been so important to us; it has come
before all else. How could we handle this and stay together? We
voiced a hundred questions and had answers for none. What
would we tell our friends? What about our daughter? What about
our son's career? What if he contracted AIDS? Then there were
the neighbours, the relatives, the church—but most of all, Matthew's life. We had no idea what we should do or where we
should turn and the only person that came to mind was the family
doctor.

Matthew came home within the hour and we hugged and
cried a little. I remember telling him that love is unconditional,
that I had loved him since the moment he came into the world
and my love would continue undiminished, always and forever.
Sadness totally overwhelmed me as I thought of his life ahead. I
did not want his dreams and his ambitions to be limited by hurt
and prejudice. I remember telling him that he must always
maintain pride and dignity in himself as a human being and that
he must never for an instant think of himself as less worthy than
any other person on Earth simply because he was gay. I do not

25

understand why there is suffering in the world, or why there are the poor, the sick, the lonely, the persecuted. However, I believe, deeply and without hesitation, that in God's 'Grand Design' there are no errors; that everything has been made perfectly to a Divine plan and there is a reason for everything. I reminded Matthew that God created him just the way he was, and He loved him just the same as any other human on Earth.

My emotions were haywire. Splinters and fragments of light and dark, ever changing, never ceasing. Like sunshine and shadow playing on a prism. Such were my emotions in the spring and early summer of 1992. Nights of sleeplessness, nights of dreams and nightmares, days of anguish and despair, diarrhoea, headaches, losing myself in my work and sudden tears at unexpected moments. Flashbacks to Matthew's childhood years. A lovely, gentle child who had found a place in so many hearts. I realised my tears were not because he was gay but because he was a very dear and beautiful human being—my son. I wanted to shield him from the hurts of life and I couldn't.

Outwardly we went about our daily lives as though nothing had changed. Bob and I leaned on each other heavily and gave each other strength. He was having problems coming to terms with his son's sexuality. He expressed no anger, no violence, just a quiet sort of sadness, and I worried about him. In those early days he was so fearful that others would find out and always imagined the worst scenario.

Matthew had confided in his sister some twelve months earlier, and Rebecca, though she was only nineteen, showed tremendous maturity and good sense and we treasured her support and looked to her for guidance, and it was through Rebecca that we learned about PFLAG. It was extremely difficult to attend that first meeting: I would rather have been anywhere else in the world. The love that existed in the room on that day was overwhelming, so strong you could feel it, and for the first time I did not feel alone. I realise now that attending that meeting was a milestone, and an important step not just for me but for the whole family.

As the weeks went by Bob was able to talk more openly, especially to Matthew, and I confided in two friends at work. Their kindness and the wisdom of their words were immeasurably helpful, and I felt less fragile. Even the most violent storms end and sunshine and calm prevails. We did not sink during our brief and violent storm; we clung together and supported one another and the miracle of it all was that, during this time, before our eyes Matthew emerged as a whole person. He was happier than we had seen him in a long time. His friends developed names, identities, families and careers. We talked honestly and at length, and I bombarded him with all manner of questions about his world. Oftentimes we laughed. The love and bonds that had always held our family together were stronger. Everything was falling into perspective again. We worried less and less about everything and began counting our blessings.

I invited some of Matthew's friends to dinner one Sunday evening. They were delightful young men, well mannered and full of fun and good humour. It was a pleasure to meet them and I felt a sense of pride that my son had chosen such sincere and true friends; that he had been able to muster the enormous courage to come out to us and that he had come to terms with his life, and most of all we were delighted to witness his obvious happiness. Then Christmas came and Matthew's partner visited on Christmas Day, as did Rebecca's boyfriend. I felt joyful that all my family was together and they were happy. It was a very special time and I treasured it.

My sadness is not that my son is gay. My sadness is for the persecution, the rejection, the ignorance and the anger of the homophobic society in which we live. The gays that I have met and know are gentle, kind and gifted souls with a warm sense of humour. They bear no malice to their fellow man, and I think of some of those more famous gays in recent and far distant times throughout history who gave so freely of their gifts and talents that the world might enjoy them forever: Michelangelo, Tchaikovsky, Stuart Challender, Nureyev, Patrick White . . .

Our gay children are not burdens, they are not to be ashamed of. Instead, they are special; they are ours and they need our love and our support as they courageously find their way in life. I do not know what the future holds for Matthew anymore than I know what it holds for myself or anyone else, but as a family we savour each day and joyfully look forward to it with optimism, and as I write these lines I think of the beautiful words from *The Prophet*, written by Kahil Gibran.

*Written by a 67-year-old mother from the northern suburbs of Sydney.*

I am writing this story in the hope that it may help others. My son is now 32 years old and I am 67 years old. My husband was killed in a motor vehicle accident when Michael was twenty and my other son, Trevor, was 24, and that left me devastated.

Michael was a student at East Sydney Technical College, studying the dress design certificate course. During the following years Michael was so devoted to his study and passed with flying colours. I would now and again have a thought go through my mind as to whether Michael might be homosexual. Then the thought would go out of my mind as I would think, No, he reminds me of myself when young—so involved in his work.

Then, one day, I said to one of Michael's friends with whom he used to study, 'Do you think Michael is homosexual?' She assured me, 'Oh no, not Michael.' So I went on blindly thinking he mustn't be.

Michael went to Paris in 1988 to further his studies in dress design and after finishing studying he got a job in Paris and I was very proud.

I had the opportunity to go to Paris in 1991. At that time I had not seen Michael for three years and I was just dying to see him. We were a very close family and I couldn't wait to say hello and catch up and talk face to face instead of on the telephone. I met Michael at the hotel I was staying at and it was so wonderful to put my arms around him and give him a great big hug.

That night, after I had been out with Michael for a wonderful dinner, he said, 'Mother, I want to meet you tomorrow on your own and have a coffee with you.' I thought, Oh, how wonderful. Michael is going to tell me he is getting engaged to be married. I imagined this because I had seen photographs of Michael with a young lady, however I was soon to learn, as mothers are wont to do regarding their children, I was putting my own interpretation on the matter.

So on Sunday afternoon, feeling extremely happy with what I thought I was going to hear, we sat across the table with coffee to hand. It is so clearly embedded in my mind. Michael said to me, 'Mum, I have something to tell you.' I said, 'Well, Michael, what is it?' Michael said, 'I am a homosexual.' With that I jumped up from out of my chair, put my arms around him and said, 'Michael, I love you very much and you are the same today as you were to me yesterday.' We cried together.

After a while I had this terrible feeling of being cheated and anger welled up inside me and I asked 'Michael, why didn't you tell me sooner?' He said, 'Mum, I was frightened of rejection,' and I said, 'Michael, my dear, you don't know me.' I felt very sad and lonely as I was with a male friend on this trip and I wished Michael's father was alive to share this with me. I went sightseeing around Paris for three days and adjusted to this news, still feeling hurt that he had not shared it with me before he left Australia.

I met the young man Michael was with, Phillipe, and what a nice person he was. I put my hand in his and shook it warmly. We met Phillipe a few times and I said to him, 'Phillipe, have you told your parents?' He answered, 'No, I can't. They would not understand.' I said, 'Phillipe, tell them.' I don't believe he ever did.

Michael and Phillipe are not together now but I am still friends with Phillipe and will always hold a little piece of love in my heart for him because he was so nice to me then, at what was such a troubling time for me.

When I arrived home from my trip, my son Trevor could tell I was angry inside for Michael not telling me of his homosexuality and he told me he had found out about a contact organisation for parents of homosexuals. I rang one person and she said I was coping quite well in her opinion.

It is five years now and I don't hide that my son is homosexual. When I arrived home from overseas I rang my twin sister and arranged to go over to her home and told her about Michael's being gay. Both she and my brother-in-law were very loving and caring to me. I went to all Michael's cousins and my older sister and told them I felt I had nothing to hide.

I can only say: I love them. Share with them. My son is so caring. When I ring Paris different friends say to me my son is a wonderful man and when he comes home to Australia to visit I hear the same from his friends here.

There is something about a lot of homosexual people that speaks of an attitude to life that others don't have. That something is invariably a heightened sensitivity. A sensitivity to feelings, experience, beauty.

So, we can go through life and learn a lot. Don't have a closed mind. Homosexuality is not a choice. My son was born one and I love him very much.

*Written by Isobel from Perth. Isobel is a 65-year-old mother of four and grandmother of seven. Born in a wheatbelt town in Western Australia, her family were pioneers of the area. She says, 'A belief in God has always been of great importance. As the Bible says "What does the Lord require of you but to do justice, and to love kindness, and to walk humbly with your God?"'*

When my son told me he was gay, I said, 'I always thought you might be.' You see, I always knew he was a special person and had an extra dimension to his personality. After he broke off his engagement to a very nice girl I again thought that he may be gay. It did not alter my attitude towards him after he told me he was homosexual, but my first emotion was of great sadness because society would not always be kind and respectful towards him. I realised that life was not going to be easy for him and he would suffer many hurts. I sat down and wrote him a letter to tell him how much I loved him.

My sadness stayed with me for a long time. I was so afraid of the future for my son and I wanted him to be happy. I felt terribly lonely and hesitated to share my sadness with the outside world. I would not have coped with people who laughed at my son or sneered at him or found him unacceptable.

One day I shared my feelings with a complete stranger when we were on a tourist bus. Attempts to talk to people who were members of my church was usually met by stony silence. This is still the case sometimes and some are still happy to tell me that they do not like homosexuality even though they know I have a gay son. However, two of my ministers have been supportive.

It was the first time I realised that there was hypocrisy in the Christian church. They preached about love and acceptance, but I realised in many cases that was only if you thought as they did and interpreted the Scriptures in the same way as they did.

I felt a terrible anger towards the church and it was a long while before I came to accept that their attitudes came from fear, wrong teaching and complete ignorance. Unfortunately they did not want to rectify any of this. I am glad that changes are taking place in the Christian church now. We may have a long way to go, but many lay people and those in higher positions are trying hard to change attitudes of discrimination and non-acceptance.

Our son is a happy man in a long-term relationship. I think of his partner as I think of my other sons-in-law, with great love and pride. We have holidayed with them and have stayed in their home on many occasions and have had the most blessed and happy times together. I am sorry they will not be parents and have the love and happiness that children bring to the home.

I still feel very angry when I hear of the biased and very nasty attitudes of homophobic people. Anger is so self-destructive to everyone, including myself, and I have learned to try and keep calm. Many people find homosexuals' lifestyles hard to deal with. These people certainly have a problem and need some help.

The people I feel close to are those who have gay offspring. We are like brothers and sisters and I can share with them a lot of my thoughts, my hurts and my anger. My son introduced me to another mum, who is now my friend.

Bishop John Shelby Spong wrote in one of his books, 'The people are here to do the loving and God is here to do the judging.' I wish people would remember that.

*Written by Isobel's husband, Stan. His wife describes him as a compassionate person who has a wonderful sense of humour and enjoys the company of others no matter what their sexual orientation, creed or colour.*

In August 1983 my eldest son, then aged 28, took me out to sit with him on our front step and said, 'I've got something to tell you—I prefer men!' My reply was, 'Well, I'm sorry for you because you are going to have a tough life!' At this point my son claims that I also said, 'I'll pay for a psychiatrist,' but I have no recollection of that. In fact, looking back I am surprised that I was not surprised at my son's revelation. It is quite probable that inside I already knew.

I told my son that our relationship was firm and that there would be no change there etc. I am so pleased that is how things have evolved ever since. There was, however, one change—our son brought home his friend. We soon found him to be a charming, witty, courteous and concerned person.

Our son had worked and studied away from home for about eight years and that situation has continued. He is still with the same partner. My wife and I visit and stay over often when we are on holidays. We have met so many of their friends, most of the same persuasion, and like our de facto son-in-law, they are extremely nice people to be amongst. We feel very special in their company.

Shortly after meeting our son's partner an event occurred at the dinner table when he was visiting. My mind wandered off and almost subconsciously I found myself repeating a naughty ditty: 'The Cabin Boy was Nipper, he was a little zipper, he stuffed his arse with broken glass and circumcised the skipper.' Under the pertaining circumstances it caused a roar of laughter. Our two visitors decided it was I who needed the psychiatrist.

My wife has always maintained that just after our eldest son told us he was gay, I said to her, 'What he needs is a good woman and a good root!'

The worst problem facing gay people is the public and, even worse, the workplace discrimination. A lot of it, probably most of it, is by people who don't closely know any gay people and how they live their lives. Another sad problem is when parents, relatives and so-called friends cut themselves off from and isolate a gay person. Some make no effort to find common ground and maintain any relationship.

Further, a majority of church-involved people 'freeze off' the gays and are judgemental, even vitriolic, and yet are still ready to quote in church, 'Judge not lest you be judged!' And many extend their judgements to the families of gays! It's time for the churches to campaign and encourage a 'Get to know closely a group of gay people' movement and understand that no one would choose to be gay—it's a situation which I believe gays are born with.

My wife and I recommend to families of gays a most helpful, informative and supportive group of parents and friends who have, or are dealing with, the problems involved on finding out that 'my child is gay'. The group is PFLAG.

*Written by a mother from Adelaide. She had a Protestant upbringing and in her youth a protected life. She has been married for 31 years. Her life changed forever, for the better, when her daughter told her that she was a lesbian. That was eight years ago and she says she has grown a lot in that time. She strongly wishes society would come to understand that sexuality is a given thing, just like being left-handed or having blue eyes.*

From the time our daughter was born, I knew that she was a special child. Our first child, our son, was, of course, extra special, but our daughter—I sensed that she was special, but didn't know why at the time. She was fiercely independent as a baby, insisting on feeding herself at the table at ten months of age and was always very decisive at a very young age. From the time she could walk, she would always have a ball in her hand and everyone marvelled at her ball skills. She went on to play cricket, football and basketball whilst in primary school and represented the state on many occasions in basketball, indoor and outdoor cricket. Academically, she was also a high achiever. I often found myself thinking, Where did this child come from? She had a zest for life that was just terrific and her self-discipline was to be admired. Joanne has always had a tremendous rapport with people of all ages. Her school teachers and her piano teacher often commented to me that Jo was an exceptional child with tremendous leadership and communication skills.

I first wondered about her sexuality when she was about eleven years old as she showed no interest in anything which I classed as 'typical' of a young girl approaching her teens. When she was thirteen, I discovered a letter in her room that she had written to another girl at school. To me, it was a 'puppy love' letter. I asked her about it. She told me that they were bored in class and 'messing around'. She was mixing with girls a lot older than her with her sport and I was wondering about her relationship with one girl in particular. I actually came straight out and asked her if she was having a lesbian relationship with this girl. She assured me that she wasn't and then asked me not to tell her father about our discussion. So the subject was closed. I continued to observe her for the next few years as I was still unsure. Her sexuality was not discussed again until she was eighteen. During the years between thirteen and eighteen she had two short friendships with boyfriends and I can remember her telling me that she was not happy waiting around for boys to call, this was not what she wanted, she just wanted their friendship and that was all.

When she was eighteen, I was emptying her bedroom tidy bin and noticed a poem. Being a poetry lover myself, I read it and I was then positive that Jo was gay as the poem was a love letter written to another girl.

I spoke to my husband about this. He was most unbelieving as he had never wondered at all about Jo's sexuality. I decided to write her a letter as when I speak from the heart I often cry, and I wanted to do this right. So I wrote the letter, asking Jo if she was gay and throughout the letter expressed our love for her. I gave her the letter when her father and brother were out for the evening and after she read it we talked.

'Yes Mum, I'm gay.' Even though I was expecting this, when

the words were actually spoken I was shocked. Jo was very defensive—she didn't know what my reaction would be and told me later that she was very frightened that we would 'kick her out of the house'. I can remember her telling me that there were heaps of homosexual people and that it was no big deal. I can also remember thinking, You must be kidding, this is a bloody big deal. We talked for hours, hugged one another and cried and cried. We connected on a deeper level, more closely than we had for a long while.

When my husband came home I told him and we cried together. He then went to Jo's room as she had gone to bed. He held her and they cried and talked for a couple of hours. This was the first time in about three years that they had touched as Jo had over the last few years become very sullen, withdrawn and quite rude to us all, but in particular to her father. She explained to us later that she was frightened of her father's reaction to the news that his only daughter was gay.

Jo told us that to come out to us was such a great relief—to have this huge load lifted from her heart and not have to lie to us ever again.

From that day on we had our daughter back and we rejoiced in that. Our family life returned to the loving, warm, honest relationship that we had all enjoyed when she was a youngster.

However, even though our love was unconditional, we were devastated. All our plans and dreams for our beautiful daughter were not to be. No grandkids. She would be lonely. She would suffer prejudice. What did we do wrong? My husband and I had a lot of issues to work through and it was not an easy time, but we made up our minds straightaway that we owed it to Jo to learn all we could about homosexuality and we made sure that all of her friends—gay or straight—were very welcome in our home.

I found that I had an urgency in me to tell someone, so I told a close friend and to my delight her response was, 'So what? It makes no difference to me.' As time has passed I have found it easier to tell people.

My husband and I have learned that homosexual relations are based on exactly the same things as heterosexual relationships and we all search for that special person to share our life with. I firmly believe that sexuality, whether gay or straight, is something we are born with. For all these people that believe homosexuals choose to be gay, I ask them—when did you consciously make a decision to be attracted to a person of the opposite sex? It is just something within us that happens—it is not a conscious thing, it just is!

We have supported our daughter from that time on and have shared her life, her loves, her ups, her downs. We have been there when her relationships have broken up, to pick up the pieces, loving and supporting her just as we have for our son. We have made some very special friendships with Jo's girlfriends and have earned the respect of all of her gay friends.

My husband and I feel blessed that we have had the experience of having a gay child as it has opened our eyes and expanded our lives to greater dimensions, and our bonds of love and support between the family unit of my husband, myself, our son and our daughter is stronger because of it.

Whilst we feel blessed, Jo has suffered discrimination and has explained to us that it is really tough being gay. She is looking for that 'someone special' in her life and although she has many friends, she still suffers from extreme loneliness, not wanting to go home alone after a night out.

We worry about her being caught up in the club scene, which she doesn't really like and becomes really tired of. She just wants a normal, quiet life, and she wants to share it with someone she cares deeply about.

My greatest wish is that prejudice against homosexuality will one day fade into oblivion.

God bless our beautiful gay children!

Most helpful books:
*Straight Parents, Gay Children*
*So is it a Choice?*

*Written by a mother from Perth.*

I found out my daughter was gay about twelve months ago. I guess I was suspecting it for quite a few years as she is 28 now and over the years has not had a boyfriend, and there were other little things too. The main reason I am writing is that she was sexually abused as a child for quite a few years by a relation and I only found out about this twelve months before she told me she was gay.

I was devastated about both, and I don't know why but I am having trouble understanding about all that has happened. I feel that I let her down as a mother and am really suffering, wondering, Is she gay because she was abused and she just hates men? I asked her this but she says it has nothing to do with it as she still has lots of male friends as well. She says she doesn't hate men. She lives now with a gay female partner and some days it upsets me, other days I accept it. That is the way she is happy.

I love my daughter very much and I feel if she's happy, so am I. But I keep thinking it is my fault a bit for not protecting her when she was a child. I have tried to ask her but she gets angry so I say nothing. She says she is finally happy now that I know. She had thought my expectations of her would be disappointed.

All her gay friends are very nice people and I work with a gay man and have a friend whose son is gay. He and my daughter knew each other as children. I keep thinking that I have met and known quite a few gay people over the years. My opinion of them is that they seem to be very gentle, kind and caring people and I get angry when I hear people laugh at them, but worry what they will think if they find out about my daughter.

I hope this letter makes some sense. I am not an experienced writer, but I think it has been helpful for me just by writing it.

*Written by a 52-year-old mother of four from Sydney who has married, for the third 'and last' time, a 'very patient and understanding man'.*

*She says, 'He has to be patient to put up with me and my children with all our problems.' Her family is very important to her.*

I have always lived in the western suburbs with my family—one sister and Mum and Dad—just ordinary folk. Dad was in the RAAF and Mum was a housewife.

I married very young and had four children. My husband turned out to be a drunken brute who was very cruel to me. He died when I was 30, leaving me to raise the children on my own. I married again soon after, but it turned out to be a disaster so I divorced him and later on married a very nice man. During these years the children grew, got through school and then all got jobs.

My daughter got herself into drugs, and went her own way. The boys all turned out well. The boys are all very different. The eldest is in the Australian Army and is a real soldier; the middle boy is more conservative and has a secure job in a bank; whilst James, the youngest, is funny, sweet, kind and rather flamboyant. He went through a bit of a drinking problem but managed to work at various jobs, mainly bar work. I never in my wildest dreams dreamt that any of the boys would be gay.

We were all rolling along quite well until one night we were out having a drink. After a few drinks, James told me he was gay. He said he had wanted to tell me for quite some time, but did not have the courage to as years before I had found some mags under his bed and yelled at him and thrown them away saying he was disgusting to read them. This I cannot remember doing, as at times I guess I was too involved in my own life to be taking much notice of their goings-on.

I remember feeling a bit giddy. I felt sick, but as he was looking at me with tears in his eyes, looking for approval, I tried to smile my best smile and tell him that it made no difference to me, I loved him just the same. I do love him, he is a very lovable boy—honest, kind, true and very funny. He told me he was sorry and that he knew I would like to have more grandchildren, but there would be none from him. I do not remember much more of that night. I think I was stunned, and was trying not to say too much.

When I got home I told my husband, Mick, who took it rather well. About all he said was that he didn't care what people did in their life, as long as they were not one of those showy, noisy loud-mouth type of people, like some of the girls and boys in Mardi Gras. James told me he was gay a week before Mardi Gras. Mick taped it and we both watched it. I thought at the time that this was very unusual for Mick. But he is a very tolerant person. As long as someone is doing the right thing, it's OK with him.

The day after James told me, I thought about it all. I thought my heart would break. My poor boy. I cursed myself for being so unkind for years before. I should have been more thoughtful, I should have given him more attention. He was happy he had told me, but I did not know if I was or not. I think it is one less burden for him to carry.

How can parents hate their children just for being gay? After all, he is part of me. He looks like me. We have shared 25 years together. In fact, now I feel closer to him. I guess my attitude to gays has changed.

When he speaks of other men, and tells me about some little romance, I still feel a tiny shudder, wishing it was not true, and that maybe he would change to liking girls overnight. But I really try to laugh with him as he keeps a close eye on my reaction.

He has many friends, boys and girls, and gets on well with most people, especially at work, but I worry a lot about him. I worry still about all my kids, but especially about him, thinking of him in places I may not like him to be, and of course I worry about AIDS.

But I could never be ashamed of him in any way. There are a lot of so-called 'normal' men out there I would not like as sons. All my sons are different from each other, but I love them all and they all love me. I know that life can be very hard on anyone who is different from the rest.

He works behind the bar in a local club and only recently told some of the other workers there. He has tried a couple of times living closer to the city, once with a flatmate, but he was not happy there so he moved back to his home town again, and at present lives on his own with his cat. I feel he is happy most of the time.

For years he shared different places with a young girl whom I liked very much, and I did think they were a couple at one stage. That ended in her being quite nasty to him, and for a long time they did not speak. That made me very sad as James is very fond of all his friends.

I do not know if homosexuality is passed on, but I now know that it is not a matter of choice. James has told me he did not ask to be born this way. I had a discussion with some of my tennis ladies and they all had different views on the subject. One lady in particular said that they most certainly had a choice in the matter. I have come across a lot of disgusting men in my time and not one of them was gay. They were Aussie yobbos who could cause their families much more heartache than a gay son.

I also find now that there are so many families around with a gay child in them.

I am glad James's father is dead because I know he would have been cruel to him. A friend of my late husband, when seeing James one day, remarked to him, 'Your dad would have rolled over in his grave to see how you turned out.' That friend is very lucky I was not there to hear it. He is a drunken lout anyway.

I think society is getting a little more tolerant, but people still tend to make jokes and not accept gay people.

I shall always be there for him for the rest of my life. Up until now he has not turned up on the doorstep with a boyfriend, but I guess I shall have to face that one day as I want him to be happy and find love in his life. I do not want him to be lonely. We all want the best for our children, to find someone to be kind, true and love them. I hope he finds a pal as nice as he is.

Yes, I would have preferred him living in a 'triple-fronted brick house with a mortgage and two kids', but it was not to be, just as my life did not turn out exactly as I would have liked it to. It took me a long time to find happiness. I just want the same for my boys.

Unfortunately my only daughter took to drugs early in her life and caused me so much trouble—that only a mother of a heroin addict would understand—and is lost to me now.

My three sons are a part of me, they look like me, sing along to the same songs, laugh at the same things and I love them all.

Recently James was coming up for a few days' break. He was expected in the afternoon but his stepfather had to go. He had tried to linger a bit to see James as we had not seen him for a few weeks. Unfortunately they missed each other. I feel Mick thought James was trying to avoid him, and when I told James that Mick was sorry he missed him, James was surprised. Mick would not hurt him, he worries about him. We both know the road is tough when you are different.

No, turn my back on any of my sons, never. James would have to do a lot more than merely finding someone of his own sex appealing.

*Written by a mother from Sydney who has just turned 50. She has two children, both now at university. Apart from teaching in a secondary school, she manages musicians and plays at weddings on a regular basis. She is immensely proud of both her children, who bring her joy in different ways.*

*Her son came out to her eighteen months ago. Her advice to parents is, 'Get educated, meet and talk with people, tell others. Above all, keep telling your child that your love for him or her is the most powerful force in your life.'*

Our son came out to us in an extremely dramatic way. At the age of seventeen he tried to commit suicide and left us a note revealing that he could not live as a 'faggot' in a homophobic world. We had never suspected that he was gay although he is very good-looking and had never had a girlfriend.

My first reaction on reading his note was concern for his health as he was in hospital. The fact that he was gay was insignificant when his life was at stake.

However, once he recovered from his attempt on his life we had to face the news about his sexual preferences. My initial question to him was, 'Are you sure?' I knew that he had no special girlfriend although he had a lot of female and male friends. I just thought that he hadn't met the right girl.

I could not have been further from the truth.

Leon explained to me that he was gay and that he would not 'grow out of it' and that it was comparable to not liking certain foods. 'You know how I don't like tomatoes,' he said to me. 'Well, in the same way, I know that I will never be attracted sexually to a woman.'

I had known gay people when I was single but as I grew older I somehow became less tolerant of what I called 'fringe groups with power'. I started to think of reasons why people 'became' gay. I have said terrible things about gay men and women. I was not just homophobic—I hated gays. My most popular theory was that it was the trend of the nineties in the Western world. It never occurred to me that BEING GAY WAS NOT A CHOICE. As I am an extroverted person, I would always voice my opinion in front of my children. Little did I know that my son, who had known that he was gay from the age of seven or eight, was hearing every word I said against gays and that it was cutting right into his heart. As he told me later, he didn't want to live if even his own mother thought he was bad and evil. It will take me a long time to forget the wounds I have inflicted upon my own child and it may take him a long time to regain his self-esteem.

My husband and I accepted very quickly that our son was gay because we learned from him that it was not his choice and that he would far prefer to be straight. We knew that we could not change him, nor would we try. We spent many hours talking to him and his doctor when he was in hospital. This was an extremely valuable time and we grew very close. I asked his forgiveness for the hurt I had inflicted upon him. Our son is a loving, sensitive, clever and popular boy who has an amazing insight into people. We now talk intimately of things that we both feel. It was a little harder for my husband as his background is non-Western and very conservative, but I feel that he handled it extremely well.

The most overwhelming emotion that came flooding into both of us was the love that we had for our son, as well as for our other child, our daughter. We believed that with such love as we felt, we could overcome our fears, our prejudices and our phobias.

Of course, I had nightmares about AIDS and HIV—fears that our son would become involved with unsuitable people or, in a fit of depression, have sex without taking precautions. But the same could apply to our daughter—heterosexuals can also catch AIDS. I still get overcome with anxiety for him. He suffers from depression and when he has a bout it really affects us all in the family.

While my son was in hospital I really needed to talk to people. I had contacts in the social work area and quickly made phone calls to different social worker friends. I wanted to find out what to do, where to go, how to handle this change in our family. My friends put us on to a gay psychiatrist who advised me to go and talk independently to a doctor, mainly about my anxieties and homophobic fears. However, I was able to sort out in my own mind that what I was confused about was not gays but paedophiles and also that the 'extremists' in the gay community, the ones who seemed to receive all the media attention, were in fact not representative of the majority of gays.

We joined an organisation know as PFLAG and the first meeting was a revelation. We didn't know what to expect, but I was amazed at the beautiful young men that I met. They were as normal as anyone you would meet anywhere and they were so open and accepting. I could ask them anything. My son had an equally amazing time and he could not get over the openness of everyone there. People had the same fears, the same phobias as we had, and we could all discuss them together. I came away from that meeting a changed person—I came away far more tolerant and full of a new knowledge about gays.

When my son came out to his friends, which he did only after attending that PFLAG meeting, he was amazed at their reaction. All of them were accepting and most of them said, 'So what!' It gave him such relief to find that no one really cared because he was still the same lovely person.

Within three weeks I had told quite a number of our friends about our son. At first we only told the immediate family. On my husband's side, because of his ethnic background it has been and will be kept a closely guarded secret. My son and I do not agree with this reaction. My son's attitude now is that he does not care who knows he is gay. If people don't approve of him, then it is they who have a problem, not he.

I was reluctant to tell my mother about Leon as I felt she was too old and very set in her ways, not at all comfortable with the modern world. However, the news that her favourite grandson was gay did not distress her greatly. She was understanding, once I gave her a few facts about being gay. The reaction of my family and friends has been supportive—even very conservative friends have shrugged their shoulders and declared that it is the way people are born. Nothing turns people gay—it's the same as having different-coloured hair or eyes. But you have to 'pick the right time' to tell your friends.

Our son has joined a support group for young gay men and I was very impressed with the way things were set up. He had to be interviewed at first and received all sorts of really sound advice on how to handle being gay. The support groups around Sydney are really wonderful.

As Catholics we had to face the fact that the church does not condone homosexuality. But we know that Jesus above all preached love for one another so that is what we have relied upon. Rather than condemn Leon or reject him, we have to love him and support him even more. There will be times when we will be rejected by people who don't understand. He will also go through different emotions when he gets involved in relationships, just as my daughter will. He will then need our support and love even more.

I have learned a lot about myself in the last six months—mainly that I was a loud-mouthed bigot. I have found my closest friends to be far more accepting than I would have been. I have also heard horror stories about children who have been turned out of home when they came out to their parents. I have accepted my son's gay friends into our home openly, just as I would my daughter's straight friends. My husband and I are one in our solid support of Leon. We will give up any friends who condemn our son or who won't listen. Some people still believe that environment and upbringing 'turn' people into gays—I certainly did. We have come a long way—my husband and I together—and I only hope that our story will help others who feel alone or bewildered.

We were lucky—we got help immediately. We were able to talk, to listen and to learn.

*Written by a mother from rural New South Wales in her early sixties. She has been happily married for 36 years. Her two daughters are married and she has three grandchildren. Her advice to other parents is, 'Enjoy your children, straight or gay. Have fun with them—life is too short to be angry and upset because they have not fulfilled your dreams of them. They are all individuals and must be respected for this.'*

When I was asked if I could write this letter my first reaction was, 'What a great idea,' then as the days went by and I gave it more thought I would feel the tears come to my eyes as my mind went back to that period about ten years ago when I thought my world had been shattered. My son—gay. Where did I go wrong, how did I make my son like this? My guilt overwhelmed me and I sank into the depths of despair.

My husband and I both had a similar upbringing as far as our religious beliefs were concerned, both attending Catholic boarding schools. Tony, our gay son, was the youngest of four children—one older brother and two sisters—and was raised in a normal family atmosphere. He seemed a very happy, caring child, giving us no worries whatsoever. He was not interested in contact sports as his older brother was. He did play soccer one year, but at the end of each game he would have no idea or interest as to what team won the game. I gave up on soccer. The gentler side of his nature came to the fore when his school decided to accept handicapped children on a trial basis. One child would not enter the school gate unless Tony was there to accompany her. One would probably have called him a loner, but as long as he had his bike he was content.

Then came high school and the smiling face disappeared. We realised he had problems but put them down to the normal phase of adolescence. He withdrew from us, but we took that as trying to stand on his own two feet. He was struck down with a severe mystery virus in year ten. He had never been ill before. Only recently has that virus been diagnosed as Chronic Fatigue Syndrome. Tony never seemed to recover from that illness. We did the rounds of the specialist doctors; his school work was suffering. He had been a top student. In the end he was referred to a psychiatrist as he was having bouts of depression.

Finally he gave up on school and we had him admitted to a hospital in Sydney under another psychiatrist. Here they told us what the problem was: he was gay. He knew his church would reject him, but would we, his family, reject him also? How could we reject our son? Love is not like a tap that can be turned off suddenly. Wasn't he suffering enough, trying to come to terms with being homosexual? Our hearts were breaking for him—we could accept anything if only he would smile again.

Tony came home from hospital. He was not our Tony. This was a complete stranger, a dejected, unhappy, hopeless soul. We had no answers for how to cope. We all withdrew into our own worlds. Tony, his father and myself. My refuge was the bathroom. I would turn on the bath and weep. Nobody could hear me there. I shed more water than those shower taps.

One day Tony overdosed on medication. He was unconscious on the bed. What would I do? My heart was breaking—why not put him out of his misery, put that pillow over his face. Don't let him suffer anymore. Yes, these were my thoughts, but I could not do it.

During these dark days I kept going back to church, praying for a miracle. 'Just please let us be happy again,' I prayed. Standing in church one night my faith fell off me like a cloak. I asked myself, 'What am I doing here?' I felt like a hypocrite. I did what I felt the God I believed in would do. I walked away from that church never to return and went home to love and take care of my son.

Tony did all he could to make us reject him. I think he felt he wasn't worthy of our love for him. One day in particular he pushed his father to the limit. Paul turned to him and said, 'No matter what you say or do, you are our son, we love you and will always be here for you.' Quite a statement from a man of few words. I think they reached Tony, but he couldn't accept them just then.

When Tony found work in Sydney we thought it would be good for him and he would settle down and be at peace with himself, but alas that was not the case. The next two years were very trying. At one stage, for six months we did not know where he was. Was he still alive, had he been beaten up? How I grieved for my son; it was like a death in the family.

During this time I was fortunate to have the support of some close friends. My heartfelt thanks go to them for the hours they spent with me. With them, I was able to pour out all my grief and fears and to realise Tony was born gay and nothing I did could change that.

Out of the blue one day Tony rang after no contact for six months. He wanted to come home and study for his HSC. I explained he could come home on our terms—no more outbursts, we all had to live together peacefully. Tony came home, passed his HSC and went on to university. At last he had some self-respect back. The following years were not all smooth sailing as he kept getting bouts of depression, but we now realise this was due to the Chronic Fatigue Syndrome.

Tony lives and works in Sydney now. He has a partner whom we all consider part of our family. He has a wide circle of friends and when he brings them home we consider them our friends too. His aim in life is to help the young gay homeless children of Sydney. In this he has our full support.

My only regret about Tony being homosexual is that he wasted so much time coming to terms with it. I think as parents we accepted the fact well before he did. As for his brother and sisters, they had no problem with it whatsoever, nor did his extended families.

As for myself, I think I have come through the trials and tribulations a much better person. I live by the old saying, 'Judge not, lest ye be judged.' The wheel has come full circle for Tony's father and myself—he is there now when we need him.

*Written by a mother of five from Sydney. Now in her late fifties, she was born in the UK and moved to Australia in 1987. She was an*

*only child who was adopted by a loving couple unable to have children of their own. Married at a young age to her first love, she has been married happily for 41 years. She has five children—three girls and two boys—four of whom have families of their own. Her advice to others is, 'Accept your child with love. Do not judge their life or happiness for we are all individual people with our own path to walk.'*

I'm sure most parents find it a shock to discover that the son or daughter they have great plans for one day, the child that will give them grandchildren, is gay.

I remember so clearly the day my son told me. I had a feeling that something was on his mind for a day or two as he was rather quiet, but thought he'd tell me what it was when he was ready. But never in a month of Sundays was I prepared for what he eventually told me, that he was gay. I couldn't seem to accept what he was telling me and I said the silliest of things like, 'We'll try to get something done about it,' and that he was probably imagining it. I mean, it's something that doesn't happen to your family, only to other people.

But I soon realised that he had carried this information for quite some time but didn't know how to tell us. As he said himself, it felt like a great burden had been lifted off his shoulders. Of course my husband was shocked and upset as was the rest of the family, his three sisters and brother, but after the initial shock we realised he hadn't changed. He was still our son and their brother, and we still loved him, so we'd get over this. I think the worst part was telling relatives and friends, some of whom looked disgusted and to this day find themselves uncomfortable in his company, and then those who have accepted the situation and it has made no difference.

All this was 22 years ago, when he was sixteen years old. He met his partner and they've been together sixteen years now. We all emigrated to Australia from England and all settled into our own lifestyle. My son and his partner have a beautiful home and have made many nice friends in the same position as themselves. And really nice guys they are. We have had some good holidays with my son and partner and have felt no embarrassment in being in their company.

They both enjoy the nieces and nephews and often have them for the day at their home or they take them out on trips. So really it hasn't changed our lives or theirs—I still have my son and I think there's a special bond between us. Other than his three sisters, I guess I'm the only woman in his life.

So all I can say to other readers and families who have to face this situation, please don't turn against them, they're still your flesh and blood no matter what. Accept it as we have done and stay together as a family.

*Written by June Smythe from Perth. June is a retired book keeper in her late fifties. She says her life has not been easy, but having overcome some really difficult times, she now feels at peace.*

It has been seventeen years since I realised my daughter was gay. She was twenty years old when she told me. I can honestly say I was very upset because as I was growing up I had been told and also picked up on the line of thinking that lesbians were like prostitutes, people you just didn't want to have anything to do with.

However, I can say I did not form any opinion about gay men because one of my friends was a Qantas steward and when I was eighteen or so he would bring his gay friends home to meet us, and I accepted them very well. In fact I liked them very much because they could relate to me emotionally and we had long talks together.

Jonnine, my daughter, seemed to be like every other teenager. My marriage broke up when she was seventeen, so the environment she was living in wasn't a good place for any role models. When she told me she was gay I really thought it was my fault because of what went on in our home. I have come to realise this is not why she is lesbian. I've been counselling parents and gay people for seven years now and have discovered that families are so varied. Most gays and lesbians come from quite 'normal' backgrounds.

I kept my feelings to myself and told Jonnine it was OK with me, I loved her whatever she was or did. I trusted her totally; she was a good person and had never caused any trouble for anyone. However, she seemed to get into relationships with partners who hurt her. I now realise I did the very same thing myself, only with the opposite sex. That was something we both had to work on, and we have over the years. Our relationship today is very loving and non-judgemental.

As for my son, Duane, he switched off in his teenage years into music and became devoted to it. I believe Duane was born homosexual. I also believe my father had problems with his sexual identification. So I believe homosexuality is genetic except for a very small percentage who are abused as children.

Duane had lots of girlfriends as a teenager, and that is exactly what they were, friends. He seemed to be asexual, not being intimate with either sex. He left home when he was seventeen, so I really didn't know what he was doing with his personal life.

When he was 21 he left for a trip around Europe and then to go and work in London. For a time he was very homesick and wrote regularly. Then after about two years he stopped writing or ringing and I became concerned that something was wrong so I decided to go to London.

This was not a good move as he was only coming to terms with his sexuality himself. I arrived and his best girlfriend said to me, 'Of course you know Duane is gay, don't you?' Well, this knocked me because I had no idea until I reflected back to his childhood, and I see now it was always there, he was different. When he was fifteen it was not unusual for him to go to the theatre by himself to see all sorts of plays—the other boys just didn't do that. He also hated contact sports and was very sensitive.

That night when he called at where I was staying he could see I was very upset and said, 'Oh God, I shouldn't have told Tanya to tell you.' It seems he was afraid to tell me because of the way I reacted to Jonnine. So the time I had there was awkward and unhappy for both of us. However, this has all changed. Duane has been back to Australia since and we have talked and we are also in constant contact by phone or postcard. I recently spent three months in London and had a wonderful time meeting all of Duane's gay friends and he is very happy and in a relationship with Martin, who is a lovely man. We even went away together for a week, just the three of us, and had a great time.

I would be lying if I said I'm not sad about never having any grandchildren, but they are the expectations I put on them. It is, unfortunately, something parents do with their children; it is handed down from generation to generation.

Today I wouldn't have it any other way. I have so many friends I have met through the gay community and I love them all. In 1985 I joined an organisation in the US called PFLAG and many parents wrote to me and gave me great love and support. I was listed in the directory as the only parent of a gay child in Australia.

In 1989 there was a Bill introduced in Western Australia's Parliament by the state Labor party to decriminalise homosexuality and I went to Parliament House to listen and support the gay law reform. Before that, I met a couple called Margaret and John who got my name from an author in the US. We met and decided to start PFLAG in Australia, which we did in December 1989, having our first meeting in Margaret and John's home. At the time the Bill was going through we did a lot of work lobbying politicians, and two Liberals crossed the floor, allowing the Bill to be passed after going through the Upper House.

Then I decided we needed a proper venue for the PFLAG meetings, so I found a place in Cottesloe and we met there once a month. We worked very hard distributing flyers and getting our literature together. We had Margaret and John and myself, and also another mother called Heather who is well known in New South Wales these days. We were available to talk to parents and gay people about coming to terms with their sexuality and soon we started a library. When I went to look for books seventeen years ago there were none anywhere. Most of the books we purchased were published in the US.

We appeared on TV and radio and we were amazed at the prejudice which is still out there. Over the years I have spoken to hundreds of people and I have many stories to tell. Only last year I resigned as president of PFLAG, but I am still an active member. In 1991 Heather's husband was transferred to Sydney and she started PFLAG over there. Today, there is a chapter in most capital cities in Australia.

When I was in London I was surprised there was no PFLAG there, only a small group outside London who meet once every three months.

Our newsletters are distributed to all the relevant groups in Western Australia and all over Australia. Our membership is up and down because people come and go, however we continue to help the gay community in every way we can, which has been very fulfilling for me especially.

We march every year in the Pride Parade in Perth with our banner which says 'We love our gay children'. We go to all the fund-raising functions the gay community have and support them in every way we can.

I will close by saying I do not think there will be any great change in people's attitudes until something is introduced into teachers' training regarding the percentage of gay children who go through the school system being bashed and taunted. There is a need for something in the high schools that the school counsellor can give these children. A great number commit suicide because they are not accepted by their peers, or at least think they aren't. Teachers have confided in me regarding help for gay children in their teens when I have been speaking at high schools on another subject.

Live and let live.

Most helpful book:
*My Son Eric*

*Written by a father from Melbourne who has three daughters and two sons, one of whom is gay. He has spent most of his working life in the advertising world as an ideas man, copywriter, marketing consultant and newspaper representative. He believes that religions create a culture of confusion and cover-ups. His sister has one homosexual son, and he has a homosexual grand-daughter.*

Afterwards, you feel so ashamed of being so dumb! The signs were there, many of them, but it takes years to accept the fact that it can happen to you. It can't be true, it can't be true, I know I can forestall it. I'll tell him it will go away, just a fancy.

But it makes no difference in the end when your son finally, and now quite forcefully has to say, 'Dad, I'm gay.' The shock was frightening to me. I burst into tears and said, 'Why didn't you tell me earlier, so I could help you through it?' He'd been trying for years to get through to my single-cell brain and I'd said a dumb thing like that at the very moment when he needed me. I was attempting to transfer responsibility. That was seven years ago and I still feel like a failure when I reflect on it.

I have always loved him as much as a father can love his son, as much as anyone can love. This may have intensified that love. Nothing can intervene in our relationship; but in my solitude I still suffer and I will do so right up to the grave—a continuing refusal to accept the fact overtly. This is my secret. Several times a week, just before sleep releases me, I weep and curse and condemn. I weep with self-pity, curse Him for the condition, and condemn our society for attaching to my son some sort of evil because his genes are of the minority sort; that our bigoted society would paint my wonderful son as a part outcast; that the ignorant among us give snide looks, knowing nods, saying so nastily, 'Well, we know what he is, don't we!'

I defy anyone in the world to find a more decent human being, a cleaner, more loving man than my gay son; and while I curse Him (because I don't know who else to curse), I truly thank Him (me being a bigoted agnostic, too) for allowing my son to have an equally wonderful partner. This partnership is the envy of many homophobics—not that they'd admit it openly. Their eyes tell me their story. It's disbelief, yes, disbelief. Of course, that's quite satisfying to see.

But who can see into my heart—the disappointment of a father's expectations, the hope that his son could enjoy the same fulfilment his father enjoyed with his mother, and now and again the disappointment to not have grandchildren, and to cry again for him because he is not properly accepted in some places because he's gay? Jesus Christ, what gives in this stinking rat-hole we call our world when ignorance and bigotry can do this to a handsome young man!

And then I begin to wonder. Am I sorry for myself or for him, or a good dash of both? Does he feel the hurts I see and feel and how does he feel about it? Does he want to hurt the hurters as I do? Does he notice the winks and the nods and the fawning declarations of mock understanding when they don't really understand a damn thing about it, the insincere lip-service, the quick subject change?

And every new or renewed encounter with friends old and new brings repeats of the same platitudes, the unspoken hurts, the winks, the nods, the turning aside.

Are there any answers to self-condemnation, self-pity? Are there any ways to help gays to survive the sneers of their fellow man? Must they remain isolated as though they are untouchable? Why cannot our irrational society see that gays are as much a part of our society as anyone else and equally capable of every human emotion? Why this absolute dichotomy? Freedom and happiness—do they not deserve an equal share? Or is the schism being built up by the exhibitionist Sydney Gay Mardi Gras, to be allowed to make them look ridiculous, to show that even they believe they are peculiar?

The fatalism of Omar Khyam offers some relief, pathetically:

*Ah, my beloved, fill the cup that clears*
*Today of past regrets and future fears—*
*Tomorrow? Why, Tomorrow I may be*
*Myself with Yesterday's Sev'n Thousand Years.*

Bewildered. Alone, with questions and no answers.
A private man.

*Written by Glenda, who is from Western Australia. Glenda and George have been married for almost 35 years. They are third-generation wheat and sheep farmers, and have always lived a very quiet life in a small district in rural Western Australia.*

We happen to be parents of a 'straight' daughter and two gay sons; our daughter is the eldest of the three.

We learned for sure of our elder son being gay in 1989, and fifteen months later we found out that our younger son was gay also. On learning of our sons' gayness, one thing was quite clear: no way were we ever going to turn our backs on them. We love all of our children unconditionally and we were in this together as a family.

Until then we were ignorant and naive, knowing nothing about homosexuality. At the beginning we were absolutely devastated and did not know how we would survive as individuals, and as a family. We felt that everything in life was stacked against us—society, and especially the church, and we couldn't see any place for us in the world.

We were desperate to read and learn about homosexuality, but we couldn't find anything at all to help us. The little we found wasn't at all educational, and we were afraid to talk to anyone about our gayness. We didn't know about the Gay and Lesbian Counselling Service in Perth. I knew we weren't alone in this, that there were many other families living with gayness, but how were we to find them?

As a mum, my greatest need was to meet and talk to another mum. We were very fortunate indeed that at this time Margaret and John, with their son and his partner, had their photo and story in the *West Australian* newspaper, titled, 'The Crime of Being Different'. This had a tremendous impact on me and it was such a comfort to read their heart-warming story. It was such a blessing that our eldest son already knew Margaret and John through the Metropolitan Community Church, and he put us in touch with them.

Through Margaret and John, we have discovered and read many very good books, and John's supply of literature has been simply marvellous. Our gay books have pride of place on our bookshelves.

Living quietly in the country, I have found that reading and learning about homosexuality has really opened up the way for me. The news of our gayness spread through the diocese of the church we belonged to. Our family was very active in the church at that time, and had organised two church camps in our area.

Our three children also organised and ran a combined church youth group in town.

We were ostracised by people in the church, people who had been close friends, including the then local minister and his wife. One man who at the time only knew of our eldest son being gay, asked our daughter and younger son to leave his home. They were visiting his teenage children who were close friends of our family; they had stayed in our home and travelled with our family to church camps. Sadly, we have all turned away from the Anglican church. It could and should have been a sanctuary for all of us at our time of need, but it wasn't.

Through our elder son, we met a very special man, at that time pastor of the Metropolitan Community Church, the Reverend David McAuliffe. He has taught me so much in giving me an insight and understanding of homosexuality. He has been a tremendous help and support to George and I and our family, especially at the most difficult times, and it meant everything to us knowing he was there to help our boys at their time of need. Not only has David helped our sons but countless other gay people as well.

It was very rewarding for us to attend the Metropolitan Community Church and to learn that God doesn't have any trouble loving gays. We were also very lucky indeed that PFLAG had just been formed in Perth. After some months we finally made a special trip to Perth to attend. It was so good to meet other parents, and this was a real breakthrough for George. The support group was our lifeline and so very important to us. Because of distance we haven't been able to attend or be involved as we would like to be. Living in the country, we are isolated in our gayness and not able to talk to any other people in the same boat as us. It means a lot to us knowing the support group is there, and only a phone call away. We're always pleased to receive our PFLAG newsletter.

We have a special bond with the friends we have because of our gayness. Our contacts are few and far between, but whenever we meet or talk on the phone we are able to pick up the thread from where we left off. We speak much from the heart, with honesty and openness, and can truly be ourselves. I am able to feel that we are not alone, and that it's OK to be gay, and that we do belong and have a right to be here.

As time went by, we decided that we wanted our closest friends and some relations to know of our gayness, so we gradually told these people. I found that writing a letter, telling our story and including some literature was the best way for me to deal with it. As the years have gone by we realise that there has been little understanding and acceptance. We have all been deeply hurt when our boys have been excluded from invitations, and when their names are not mentioned and they're not asked after. It's like people pretend they do not exist.

As a family, we don't have any extended family life at all, and it means that our family is small, and very lonely, especially for our boys. People who have large extended families, and love within their families, don't know how lucky they are—but for the grace of God, they could be in our situation. We have a special place in our hearts for the dear people who care for, and accept, our boys just the same as they did before knowing of our gayness.

From my research and contact with others, I know that gayness is very much a family matter, and when there is one gay member in a family, it is not unusual to have other gay members in the family, with extended family having gays in the closet. In some families, including ours, there have always been gays.

Life has never been easy for us and all along this gayness struggle has been part of that, even though we weren't aware of it. Since we have known, I can honestly say that our family has been to 'hell and back'. Many times our family falls apart. It has been a struggle for our daughter, coming to terms with having two gay brothers. Being part of a small country town, through work and mixing socially, there has been little understanding and acceptance. Society is conditioned in its thinking. There is such a stigma to gayness, and gays are constantly the butt of cruel jokes, and I am continually deeply hurt by this and treat them with stony silence.

Of course there are times when we feel sad, and understandably so. Our boys have left their life here on the land with us and made new lives in the city and interstate. Being gay, they would not be accepted in the small, country community. We always had the idealistic view that our family would make their lives here on the land, close to us, and we had the hope of having lots of grandchildren too. However, that was our dream, not that of our sons. It is difficult for us to fill this void we have in our lives. Farming is the only life we know and with just the two of us left here to cope with the workload, we know that eventually our land will be sold. In the meantime we have to face the very difficult decision of when, and where, we will move on to live.

It can be a cold, cruel world out there for so many gays. Sadly, they are faced with so many difficulties. After suffering so much in coming to terms with their homosexuality, they so often have to live with the rejection by family and friends, as well as difficulties in their workplace, fearing for their safety, and also living in fear of the law. Gays have been gaoled, the only crime their being born homosexual.

Many gays have a very sad story to tell, some live with HIV and most have experienced losing someone they know and care for to AIDS. Our lives have been touched by having friends with HIV, and the suffering and sadness caused by a death from AIDS, and the death of a family friend by suicide—I miss his voice, and phone calls—he will always be remembered. So sad, and such a waste of a life. Being born gay is no different than being left-handed; no one would ever choose this path in life, it is too difficult.

Being born gay is not a 'sin', the true 'sin' is when parents, families and society cruelly reject a person who happens to be gay. I cannot understand how they can do this; they ought to be thoroughly ashamed of treating a fellow human being in this way. Gay men generally are very caring, loving people who contribute much to society. It is a privilege for us to meet and mix with them, and many have become very dear friends. Some of our most enjoyable times have been spent with our family at gay venues in Perth, dancing with gays and lesbians, and receiving their response in return to us for being there. I am very grateful to John for his marvellous collection of literature handouts. He keeps me in good supply, as do our support group when needed. It is very rewarding for us to be able to reach out to gays and give them literature handouts for themselves and their families, and in doing so, putting them in touch with our support group, with the hope that it will be as helpful to them as it has been to us. From our little corner of the world here on our farm, I've been able to send literature to different parts of Australia, as well as overseas.

It is good having our phone number listed as the country help-line, and knowing that the calls I have received have made a difference to someone needing to talk about gayness.

We are richer for having two gay sons, men who anyone would be proud to call their own. We have a closeness with them that we would never have had if they had been born 'straight'. We love their friends and partners as our own; they are our family and are welcomed and stay in our home.

We hope and pray that in the future the world will be a better place for all gay men, lesbians and their families, and that we can in our own quiet way work towards this in the years to come. A very special thank you to Margaret and John for paving the way for us, and also to our very dear friend David McAuliffe.

*Written by a mother from rural Queensland.*

We adopted a boy when he was one year old. Not that we needed to as we already had six children born to us, but we wanted to take a child who was not quite perfect, one who needed special care. We were anxious to adopt as soon as possible. It took two years to legalise it nevertheless. What a dear little fellow he was, very gentle and the exact opposite of our natural-born child, Emma, who was four months older. The welfare department had made a mistake in placing our son with us as it is policy to have at least fifteen months between children. I pleaded to keep him. Emma had a very strong personality, a perfect child, but when she was two years and nine months she succumbed to a virus and was taken from us.

James, our eighth child, came soon after so we had two babies to replace the one we lost. Our 'chosen' child, who will remain nameless, was slow. He didn't walk until he was two. He'd never crawled, getting along by sliding on his bottom. He wore out so many pairs of pants! Now, I don't know whether any of this had any bearing on his behavioural problems. If you notice a crawling child, every part of the body moves. It has been discovered that if a child doesn't crawl, part of the brain may not be stimulated, so other parts become stronger. He never reasoned quite like the other children; in some ways he almost seemed more advanced. When he was twelve he had body hair with early onset of puberty. He could have starved, so many of his hormones were overworking. He was always a loner and seemed to admire boys at school who were popular and excelled. We had to tell this to his teacher, as there was one teacher for several age groups, being a country school. He was so well behaved he'd be overlooked, so the teacher made an effort to draw him out.

He was never invited to birthday parties like our younger son was. He was less outgoing and popular. So I would ask his friends home and he always mentioned one special friend, but he was never able to come. I don't know if there was another reason, but the excuse was always that his friend was too busy playing sport etc.

We had a clinic and a practitioner lived on the premises. One day the practitioner's wife said our son touched her boy where he shouldn't have. A 'former' gay fellow, professing to be cured, found out about this and singled out our son as someone he could help. He talked us into going to a session at the Anglican church he attended, where they were dealing with these issues.

I also took our son to the hospital to see a psychiatrist to have him assessed. The doctor said he liked both sexes, but he only seemed to be friendly with girls. I presume this was because of his gentle nature. The doctor's passing remark was, 'The best of British luck to you.' We also had him checked at the time for HIV. The doctor, a woman, said to me, 'You know you'll have to accept the way he is and learn to live with it.' I turned to her and said, 'If it was your son, would you be happy?' She stammered and said, 'Well no.' I said, 'Exactly.'

We tried to find out if he'd been interfered with as we'd heard this could trigger off this behaviour. He'd had a fascination for public toilets. We lived near the beach, and he said there was a man who approached boys sitting alone. I did some detective work. So did my older sons. We actually tried to intercept this man. But our son's story always changed; he'd become untruthful, saying it was other men. One day I sat apart from him and waited to catch the culprit. It was a very hot day, there was no shade and I sat with a towel over my head for several hours . . . nothing happened.

We didn't get any reports from our son's school, but one day a lad came by our house and said he was gay and he knew our son was. It was like he was dobbing him in. We tried to tell our son that he need not be stuck with it, but at the back of my mind was always this nagging uncertainty that our son may not be able to help it. When he was seventeen we were contacted by the local courthouse. He'd been charged with offensive behaviour in a toilet. He had propositioned a policeman! For eighteen months we needed to see that he fronted up to a counsellor once a fortnight. This councellor was hopeless. Counselling was just a job to him. He looked like a heavy drinker and he blew smoke at us.

Our son just missed out on criminal charges because he was underage. Because he was eighteen, we were not told about the outcome of the psychiatrists' findings. We felt this was a bit unfair, being his parents. We had our son pay for his appointments but he only had two. He said he didn't need any more.

It was a shock to find he was still 'not right'. What followed was a few years of stealing and lying, and when our daughter moved into a flat, he went with her. He came home to live on and off, but preferred to flat with girls. Then when we bought a farm for the second time and left the coast he took off to Brisbane. He frequents gay bars and lives with a young man, but this young man has a girlfriend. He shaves his legs now and again, saying it is cooler. We've kept the door open and he knows we all love and care for him. He admitted only recently he'd been touching his nephews when young, but only experimentally.

I know it is an acquired lifestyle and as such can be overcome. Read the Book of Romans. Our son overcame his being slow in developing. He was a crack swimmer and could have excelled. Now he doesn't play sport, has become overweight and sleeps too much. We hope and pray he will turn his life around and become what he is meant to be. We found his mum when he was seventeen but she is in a nursing home and she didn't want him to see her. At 41, being unmarried and quite sick, she chose to bring him into the world and not have an abortion, so there was love there. I was 43 when he came to us. My husband has been very good. He may have accepted it better because our son is not 'blood', but it can happen to anyone.

We are alternative in our approach to life. My husband of 43 years had a nervous breakdown at 39. We had already had four children. Neither of us were particularly religious at the time but we were in great need of help. My dad prayed for the first time when he was diagnosed with cancer. Why do we only pray in desperation? All we need to do is speak to our Father as we talk to anyone. I guess it's just that we can't see Him in the flesh, but we can feel his spirit and the 'still small voice'.

Getting back to becoming alternative, we tried conventional methods of healing, which didn't work, and as I prayed the answers came. I couldn't understand why my husband would succumb to nerves. He had inherited the weakness from his mum. I'd thought our life was pretty good. A home, work, a good marriage and four healthy children. A friend of my daughter's had been to Hopewood, a health-care centre at the foot of the Blue Mountains in New South Wales, which prescribed fasting, natural foods, fresh air, sunshine and a positive mental attitude. To cut it short, the laws of nature need to be followed or we're in trouble. A 'word of wisdom', if you like, to keep our bodies free from harmful substances such as alcohol, tobacco and drugs, but more importantly, to follow the laws of God. To break these laws is to experience great sadness.

They are very simple laws, not for academics or wise men only, but for the meek and lowly—it's intelligence, really. The Pope has said the sin is not in being homosexual but in what homosexuals do to abuse their bodies, which are the temples of the Lord. Speaking of temples of the Lord, take a ride to Carlingford in Sydney and you will see a bricks-and-mortar temple. Therein are performed sacred ordinances which bind us to loved ones as well as teaching us the mysteries of life—where we come from, what we are doing here, where we are going. You can't ask for any more than this.

*Written by Kath Kean, a mother of five from Nowra, New South
Wales. Kath is a community welfare worker. She dabbles in the theatrical
arts, writes essays and plays bridge. She is also a volunteer carer with
Community Support Network (CSN), looking after people with
HIV/AIDS, and is a member of PFLAG.*

I was taking an afternoon siesta when Andrew came in, jumped
on my bed and said: 'Mum, I've got something to tell you.'

I sighed. Bringing up three rowdy teenage boys in the country
on a pension was no picnic and I wondered what had happened
this time.

'It has taken a lot of courage to tell you this, Mum.'

'OK, Andrew,' I replied. 'Who did what?'

'No, it's not like that. Mum . . . um . . . I'm gay.'

After my divorce I had become determined that my sons
would grow up in peace and harmony, with no strict rules, but
with freedom of thought, privacy and respect. Because of this,
our communication skills improved out of sight and a wonderful
camaraderie developed between us, along with their two adult
sisters who had flown the nest.

Gay! He thinks he's gay! I remembered discussing this very
situation with a friend once. He asked me how I would react if
one of my kids told me he was gay. I didn't know. I had nothing
against gays. In fact, I had known a few in my time and had very
good rapport with them, but I hadn't thought about one of my
children being gay and I honestly didn't know how I would feel
about it.

Gay! He had three schoolfriends who were gay. He told me
about them and asked if it was all right if they came around
sometimes. Of course, I didn't mind. They were great kids, lots
of fun, and I marvelled at his loyalty because they were certainly
behind the eight ball among their peers at school.

'Gay! What makes you think you're gay?'

'I've known for a long time Mum. Remember that terrible
time when I was fifteen?'

I thought back. Yes, his schoolwork took a nosedive, and he was depressed for months and spent most of his time in his room.

'That's when I was coming to terms with it. I couldn't tell you because I hoped it was a passing phase.'

I searched his face and my thoughts flew back to when he was a newborn. He was my fourth child and when they placed him in my arms all wrapped up, I looked at him, as I did with the others, for that 'recognition', that inner knowledge of each other, and there was none. He looked back at me with that wise look in his eyes that newborns have and it was like we were meeting for the first time. I didn't 'know him'. Wow, I thought, Where have you come from, little one? No matter, it must have been somewhere special.

His nature was lovable and sunny, always laughing and mischievous, and his school years were happy. He grew into a real charmer, flashing his smile at teachers, who fell for him immediately, even through high school. His school reports were always glowing even when his marks were down, and when I visited his teachers, their faces lit up when they talked about him.

His childhood was normal, with the usual mischief boys get up to. Not being a sports lover, he chose music and happily went along to piano lessons, guitar and drama classes. He attempted the violin and played a pretty good recorder. The journey through teens, along with his brothers, was filled with the usual loud music, rough-housing, girls, deep-and-meaningfuls on the phone for hours, appalling jokes, gazing into the refrigerator, driving lessons and the usual chaos which goes hand in hand with pimples, hairstyles and dress sense.

Gay! But what about Melissa? 'You loved Melissa, didn't you?'

'Yes, I did, I really did and I tried so hard to be attracted to her that way, but it just didn't happen.'

Gay! He lay there waiting for my ultimate reaction, hoping that it would be all right.

After the birth of my last child I had suffered complications through a simple operation and haemorrhaged internally for ten hours.

Consequently, I experienced the five stages of dying—realisation/disbelief, fear/panic, anger, desperation and finally acceptance, all in the space of twenty minutes before I was taken back to the operating theatre. Lying there helpless, going through the first four stages was terrifying.

I was at the indestructible age of 32 and I screamed inwardly with disbelief. Then terror struck in all its force with the realisation that they were going to put me under and I would probably never wake up. I would be dead and there was absolutely nothing I could do about it. I began to fight and got exceedingly angry with God, accusing him of taking away my life without a second thought. How dare he do this to me? The anger became white hot and by the time I reached the theatre my whole internal being was crying out.

The theatre nurse was gentle with me. I remembered joking with her that morning just before I went under. She looked at me now over her mask with fear in her eyes. With great difficulty, for speech was exhausting, I apologised for dragging her out of her cosy bed. She held my hand and promised to do her best. One beautiful moment passed in silence between us.

I let her know that no matter what the outcome, it would be all right. I was grateful for her support and I was indeed supporting her in what I thought would be my finality. My struggle with consciousness was overwhelming and acceptance was beginning to dawn.

And dawn it did, like a beautiful light. I had everything to live for, youth, four beautiful children, a brand-new baby and a marriage which at the time was struggling but had a purpose. I looked down on my family and saw each one as a separate individual, each with his or her own path to follow, paths that no one could walk upon but themselves, and I knew they would be all right because each life had a purpose to fulfil. I found myself standing in between life and death: on my left was life, family and love, and on my right was home and an even greater love. I placed my fate in this greater love, stating that my destiny was in His hands and that either way, life or eternal life, at this stage of my being would be joyous. I slipped into unconsciousness and awoke several hours later to life and the four walls of the intensive-care ward. Joy.

From then on my whole life and thought process have changed. Major catastrophes became very minor ones and, over a period of time, things that I had thought were important, such as possessions, society's demands and judgements of others, quietly and naturally took a back seat.

Gay! How was I supposed to react? I thought to myself. With horror? How was I feeling? I was feeling OK. I looked at him. Had he changed? No, of course not. He was still the same rambunctious, clumsy, sunny, loving and sensitive teenager with big feet. I smiled and said: 'It's OK. You're gay and it's OK. I love you for who you are, not what you are.'

I proceeded to lecture him on the importance of looking after himself along with his self-esteem. I did have a feeling of sadness that he would possibly be rejected by society, making his life difficult, and maybe never know the joy of producing his own offspring.

How could I accept so easily? I asked myself a dozen times. Was I afraid of losing his love and respect? How do other parents react, and why? There was no way of finding out. Questioning other gays I knew, I heard horror stories of not being accepted by their families and of some even being cut off. I was determined that, no matter how I really felt, this would not happen.

Was I accepting his situation with my soul or just my intellect? The rest was to come eighteen months later. 'Mum, Warren and I have got some time off from work. Can I bring him home to meet you? Can we stay with you for a week? I'd like him to see where I grew up.'

'Of course you can.' How was I feeling now? OK. They were to arrive the following day. On my way to the guest room to make up the bed, I stopped in my tracks. My God, they're going to sleep together. Never mind your daughter bringing home her boyfriend, what about your son and his partner?

I took a deep breath. I knew they were living together, so to separate them would be ridiculous. And why would I want to if I had truly accepted him? This was his life and he had to learn in his own way. I made up the double bed.

They arrived with the usual bedlam of suitcases, hellos, kisses and an overjoyed, welcoming dog. Warren was lovely and we had a wonderful night eating and reminiscing. Finally it came time to go to bed. Without a second thought I said good night and, with a happy weariness, trotted off to slumberland.

When I awoke the next morning I realised they were actually

here and sleeping in the guest room. How do you feel? I feel OK. Hey, I feel OK! I knocked on their door and popped my head in at their invitation—no shocks, just happiness that they were there. I looked at these two as they were, two human beings who loved each other, who had much to contribute to each other and society over their lifetimes, their paths running side by side.

Their relationship was totally accepted by his brothers and sisters and even by my two very Australian heterosexual sons-in-law. Our family get-togethers are full of laughter and love. I am very fortunate.

My dying experience was real and held absolute truths. It matters not what society or religions dictate. What really matters is the development of one's soul in a positive direction. Ours is not to reason why. Judgement of our fellow beings is one of the greatest sins of all.

Andrew and Warren have now been together for seven years. Their relationship is solid and very happy, strengthened by the support and unconditional love and acceptance from our family. We count our blessings.

*Written by a retired engineer who was born in New Zealand and is the father of a daughter and a son. His son realised he was gay when he was in his late teens and has recently told him that he is HIV Antibody Positive. There has been a realisation within the family that it is important to carry on with living and to encourage the enjoyment of life with an affirming attitude.*

Why didn't we know sooner! It wasn't until he was twenty-two years of age that our son told us he was gay.

As a lad he showed great talent and consideration for others, but in his later teenage years an aggressive attitude appeared. We had witnessed similar events in other families but had not expected to face this situation ourselves; we were hurt. Showing our love seemed not to make any difference. It was a difficult time because we had been close as a family, with ourselves, our son and our daughter getting along well together; what was going wrong?

When he finally told us he was gay our first reactions were those of shock. My immediate thought was, What if he contracts AIDS? His mother wondered if in any way she was to blame and whether it would be possible to stop him from being homosexual. Our daughter was sorry she had not recognised what her brother was going through and that he had not felt able to confide in her as they had always been good friends.

Gradually we were able to talk more freely together, becoming accustomed to the fact of his sexual orientation, with a restoration of the affection we had all previously enjoyed.

Later he told us he had been raped by a man from his work. It was someone he felt safe with, who he thought would understand. Horrified by this, now we were able to lay our distress aside to be supportive.

My own previous experience of homosexuality was minimal, not having any contact with this apart from certain crude jokes, even during my war service, whether at home or abroad. I doubt if I really knew what the word 'lesbian' meant at all in those earlier years.

As our son gained in self-esteem he became once more the young man we had always loved and were used to—generous, thoughtful and loving—but we still looked for reasons why. Good friends, whose families had grown up with ours, were to tell us that they had recognised our son's sexuality before we knew about it! We were glad to have their support and we shared our concerns with them.

Australia beckoned our son, where he found a better acceptance of gays. We kept in constant touch by phone and several visits were made to and from Sydney. It was four years after our son told us that we felt able to tell his grandmother about his sexuality. After a brief silence her comment was, 'Well, he is my grandson and I love him!' Their caring relationship has never faltered.

Later, we were fortunate to meet and become friends with Terry Stewart and her husband Ron. Terry is the author of *Invisible Families*, which is highly recommended. Our discussions with them have given us a greater understanding of the problems which may face gay or lesbian people.

As members of a denomination presently discussing issues regarding homosexuality and the church, we have found many of our local members to be accepting of homosexual persons, while others with more fundamental views are very much opposed, particularly to having a gay minister taking services.

A public questions committee in our church decided on three questions as possible issues for action. One of them was 'Should we sanction the teaching of self-esteem to homosexual children in schools?' This gave me an opportunity to explain that many such children, or even those presumed to be gay/lesbian, were being victimised to a point of suicide at school.

Also, that the Ministry of Health ran an inclusive health and sexuality pilot scheme, which found acceptance by many parents. When the parish council realised that such children often knew they were different but not why, and how they hated to be different, the committee asked what could be done to make amends.

Another opportunity arose when I responded to an invitation to comment on an article in a church newsletter relating to gay ministers being able to preach in church. It reads:

> The church continues with struggles. We really should go beyond just tolerating each other and use it as a stepping-stone towards more understanding and equality. Can it be right to erect barriers against children and men and women on the basis of what they are? If gay and lesbian people have chosen to follow Christ, and because of their gifts, training and calling are ordained, then what has their sexuality got to do with their spirituality? To define Christianity so narrowly raises the type of barrier that Jesus removed.

At the age of 30, our son returned to work in Wellington for eight months. He found friends there, and this city is now a much more pleasant place for gays, due in part to New Zealand's Human Rights Act and more recent anti-discrimination law amendments.

I now ask myself, what if we stopped loving our son? Would he have committed suicide? He told us of some who had because of being denied their parents' understanding love. This has been further confirmed to us as we've become aware of other families' problems.

Of course we had thoughts of what might have been . . . a happy marriage like his sister has . . . maybe grandchildren to devote our time to? However, NOTHING could replace the affection shown to us by our boy because we were fortunate enough to have held onto our love for him.

Most helpful books:
*Invisible Families*
*The NZ AIDS Foundation Booklet*

*Written by a happily married mother of two from rural New South Wales. She and her husband raised their son and daughter on a small farm. Her advice is, 'Try to accept what cannot be changed. Love your child just the same—they are still the same person—and do not dwell too much on your own losses. Support each other and you'll all be a happy family once again.'*

I first had suspicions that my son could have gay tendencies from about twelve months prior to confirmation that he was gay, but I always used to dismiss it as 'only in my imagination'. The suspicions got worse and eventually I summed everything up and on Melbourne Cup Day 1995 while I was at work I rang him at home and said I knew. He and I cried together over the phone and he told me how much he loved me and that he had gone through twelve months of hell trying to find out if he was or wasn't—going to counsellors—ringing hotlines in major cities etc., etc. It's funny, because I was more upset at the time for him and what he had been through by himself, and us not being able to help him.

I was very concerned about my husband finding out as he was very anti-gay—the usual fatherly disgust for homosexuals—and at the time I said that I didn't want him to know. I was sick with worry, and all the usual feelings. I couldn't eat that night and had to take the next day off work to sort out what I'd do.

My beautiful son—I could not believe it! The things that went through my mind were incredible! I don't think I've ever cried so much.

After two days of dreadful nausea, anxiety and not being able to concentrate at work, I finally cracked when my husband asked if something was wrong. On the edge of a breakdown, I blurted it out! I could not believe his response. He was just so great! He broke down too for a while then pulled himself together. We talked about it and he said that he had had his suspicions too, but for many years before I did! He said we would just have to accept it and that he felt the same for him, but I don't think the shock had really set in.

I took it worse than my husband and could not stop crying. It was on my mind in all my waking hours and I could not stop thinking about it, which I think was causing the anxiety attacks. I told my closest work colleagues and my wonderful boss, who was just great; he knows all my family. I had to go to the doctor to get something to help my nerves and anxiety. I really felt like I wanted to die, that my world had ended—something inside me died. My husband was just so supportive, though—I just couldn't believe how much so. But he had to handle it in his own way, and he wasn't the same with my son as he used to be, which made me more upset. This has changed now and gradually he is becoming more relaxed and talking to him like he did before. Patience is needed, so much patience, so don't try to rush things! I never thought I'd be the same again. I ended up going to a counsellor, which was a great help. I can recommend anyone contact a counsellor—the more you get off your chest the better.

I also rang a support group in Melbourne called PFLAG and they arranged to send me literature aimed at parents. Had I not had this sent to my husband and I, I don't think he could have been as accepting as he is. It really has helped me and surprised me. I do think he was doing it for my sake, too. A lady from PFLAG told me it took her family years to accept it fully, but after only six weeks, I'm eating, laughing etc. again.

I still have my bad days, and think about what it was like before we knew and what it would have been like when he married and had children, but it doesn't hurt quite as much now.

We haven't told our daughter yet, but he wants to when he feels ready. I'm sure she's had her suspicions.

My son is very close to my sister and it turned out that he had told her quite some time ago. My sister has been so fantastic and I don't know what I would have done without her and her husband.

To all other parents—what your son goes through is so traumatic. Think of them too, be supportive, loving. Tell them you love them. I do, every day. He's still the same person as he was. The going is not easy. I really did feel that life was not worth living. I had to remind myself that I still had a beautiful daughter at uni, a mother, sisters, a brother etc. I still worry about what the future holds for my son. Thank heavens he's not one of those types who is so obviously gay and flaunting himself around. He's the most beautiful boy—kind, handsome, considerate, caring, loving etc. I look at him when he's asleep and go off for a little cry—my baby is no longer a young teenager with a prospective girlfriend, marriage etc. But knowing they are 'born' and not 'made' gay does help—naturally, we tried to think of what we may have done to make him this way, then I re-read the literature I have, which reminds me that we have done nothing.

I do hope this helps someone out there. Please don't kick them out. My son was so scared that we would. Nothing could ever make me kick my son out, nothing could ever stop me loving him as much as I do. In fact, I think I even love him more. They are still your sons and need as much support and love as they can get.

In conclusion, the 'pluses' are: it brought my husband and I closer; there are no more suspicions; I would never hold back anymore; we appreciate honesty; we do not take things for granted. Our life has changed, but we are seeing normality in it again. We've surprised ourselves that it has taken less time to feel OK and that it's not the end of the world.

We just hope and pray that our son is happy, healthy and that no harm comes to him. We'll always be there for him, no matter what.

*Written by a mother from Christchurch, New Zealand. During her training as a schoolteacher she met and married her husband, a pharmacist. They had three boys and a daughter and she now has seven grandsons and a granddaughter.*

*Her husband died in 1988. Together they had been fully involved at a local and national level in their church. She feels that her love and commitment to her God have helped and not hindered her in accepting the challenges that life has sometimes thrown her way. She says, 'Each individual is a gift from God—precious, unique, of your flesh and blood, a part of you that you cannot ever ignore. Ignore it to your peril. It will haunt you till you die.'*

How does one begin to describe one's feelings the day you are told your youngest son is gay? Where do you even begin to find the words to explain the emotions that tumble about inside one's head, one's stomach, as the words are said, 'Mum, I'm gay'?

You sit there looking at your son, hearing what he is saying, but somehow not understanding or even wanting to begin to understand what you've just been told. You can't believe what this tall, fair-haired, handsome, blue-eyed young man is trying to tell you.

You manage, through the mists, to say, almost robot-like, 'I hear what you're saying, I'm trying to comprehend what you're saying—are you sure, really sure? Are you being "led" the wrong way by those you're associating with? Is this the reason you left your girlfriend? Is it something I've done, or your father has done?' Other, equally ridiculous, questions follow.

You manage to say—and you mean it, really mean it—'You are my son, I love you and I always will. This will make no difference. Just give me time to come to grips with this. It's not something I ever contemplated coping with . . .'

This all happened the day my 'baby' turned 21. He was to have his 21st at home with family and friends. He and his father had kept the information that he had chicken pox from me. In the end he had to come out and admit it as spots appeared on his face.

We were sitting on the couch with this news when he came out with the OTHER news.

We had the party and it was then that I met up with some of the gays who love to flaunt their difference and play on it. I was upset. I hoped my lad was not like that away from home.

Here, with us, he was a quiet, caring, loving young man; a real homebody. What's he like away from home? Questions, hundreds of them, buzzing around.

His dad seemed to cope with the information better that I did. As a mother, the one who bore him, I had many questions.

I had two boys and one girl. I had wanted desperately to be like my mother-in-law and produce boy, girl, boy, girl. That would have been my aim, but when this beautiful little boy arrived, I wouldn't have changed him for anything. He was an attractive child, placid and loving. The others adored him.

Now, was it my fault because I had wanted a girl so much?

I decided the only way I could cope was to read all I could. With each piece I read, I realised it wasn't my fault, it was nature playing one of its 'twists'.

I know my young son was extremely worried about the rest of the family's reactions. He needn't have worried—their generation copes better than we oldies and they love their younger brother.

I do know my daughter is concerned about her boys' reaction. However, as they are growing, the older boys, I am sure, already understand the relationship. They know and like my son's partner.

That was another problem for me—when my son informed me of this special relationship. He told me that they had formed a commitment and were going to live together.

Another hurdle—it seemed I couldn't win. My husband had by this time died, so I had no one to talk to and mountains can be made of molehills when one is alone.

The next hurdle was actually steeling myself to take the step to travel to Australia, where they were living, and stay with them. How would I cope knowing they were in the next room sleeping together, perhaps even having sex? Wow!!!! Unbelievable what the mind can conjure up.

It proved to be a very wonderful holiday. They were very circumspect. I felt completely at ease. There was no embarrassment.

They weren't 'screaming queens'. They were young businessmen with a wide group of both male and female friends. A group of immaculate personalities with flats, and cooking skills, that would put many women to shame.

Mind you, to be honest, I really don't know how I'd have coped if he had been a 'screaming queen'!!

My son's personal life within the four walls of his flat is his business and should not be anyone else's unless it impinges on their lives.

I do remember saying to his partner during that first time I stayed (partly in jest and yet with real conviction) that if he ever hurt my son, I'd kill him.

I've relaxed since then. Life is too short. I love them both. I often holiday with them. I am proud to be seen with them, as I hope they are proud to be seen with me. They are both handsome, wholesome young men. Young men that any mother would, and should, be proud of.

There is only one thing that haunts me and that is the fear that AIDS brings to all mothers, especially mothers of gay men and women.

This whole experience has, I hope, made me a more tolerant person. I've had a 'few things' to cope with over the past few years. These have educated and matured this 61-year-old. One is never too old to learn and enjoy the experiences that broaden and make our lives full, colourful and challenged.

My message, then, to other parents is this.

Take a deep breath.

Take your time—everyone regrets decisions made in haste.

Love them—after all, they are part of you.

Remember, they never asked to be 'gay'.

Be proud of your child—it takes guts to live an 'honest' life when the world contains many ill-informed, sanctimonious people.

Love them always, no matter what.

When I think of all the dreadful things that could have happened to any of my children, I am extremely grateful.

I am one very proud New Zealand mum. Proud of ALL my children.

I pray that God will continue to keep them ALL safe, happy and healthy.

*Aroha* (love) from Christchurch, New Zealand.

*Written by Anne Gregory from Port Clinton, South Australia.*

I have insisted that our real names are used in this story because I am proud of my son and feel that we have nothing to be ashamed of and so have no reason to hide behind a false name. Not only do I feel that I have nothing to hide, I want the world to know that being gay is normal. Having a gay child can be the most interesting, loving experience a parent can have and I wouldn't have missed this experience for quids, as we used to say.

Michael came out to me when he was about seventeen. He was the youngest of three children and had an older brother and sister. He was somehow different from the other two, but then they were quite different in nature from each other too. I used to wonder how one person could have three kids who are all so different from each other. Michael was more sensitive and more single-minded. He loved the theatre, 'Dungeons and Dragons', computers, books, old people, girls, good food (ordered oysters mornay with great aplomb from the age of six) and had a wonderful zest for life. For me, he was easy to be with, a companion.

You may have noticed that I have written this in the past tense. Michael died due to AIDS in 1993. He was 25. His death taught me that if I had any residual feelings of discomfort that he was gay, they didn't matter two hoots compared with losing him. I'd like people to think about that. Death sure puts things into context for you.

Anyway, one Friday night in 1985 Michael invited me into the kitchen for 'A Talk'. This usually meant it was going to cost me money. He had a computer and a synthesiser, so I thought, Oh God, he wants a car. He fixed me with what we had learned to call 'the Michael look' and when I was settled and paying attention, he said, 'Mum, I've got something to tell you. I'm gay.' I felt my face go sort of stiff.

I had never tried to analyse my kids. They were as they were, so it had never occurred to me that Michael was anything other than a quiet, artistic, clever kid. Something went 'click' in my mind and even though I suggested that maybe he was 'experimenting with his sexuality'—Maybe you are bisexual, I thought. 'Are you sure?' I asked—deep down I knew that he was what he said: gay.

Then the panic started. AIDS was in the news, the grim reaper commercial was on TV and a man had been quietly sacked from the shopping centre where I worked when they found out he was gay. I was so afraid that Michael would be swallowed up by the predatory gay men that I had read and heard about. I was sure that no one would love him, that he would be promiscuous and that he would get AIDS and die. In a split second I had it all worked out. Then the guilt started. His father and I had separated nine years before and I had reared the children alone, therefore I must have mollycoddled him and made him 'that way'. He had very swollen breasts when he was about three weeks old due to a crossover of hormones from me, so me and my hormones were to blame!

Lucky for me, he could see what was going on. My face has never been able to keep a secret, and he proceeded to teach me about being homosexual. But before he did that, he asked me a question. The question that must surely haunt all gay and lesbian children when they finally are brave enough or desperate enough to come out to parents. He said, 'Now do you hate me?' That pulled me up short. All the negatives and garbage that were whirling around in my head vanished as I realised some of what he must have been going through for years. The silences, the withdrawal from friends and family that had crept into our home, the feeling of a glass wall between us at times that we had put down to him being a teenager, going through year twelve etc., etc. Everything fell into place. I felt ashamed of myself for my reaction. This was my son, who I loved and always would. I told him so and said that nothing, NOTHING would ever change the way I loved him. I was so sorry that he had struggled with this for so long before he could tell me.

When I look back at those times, I realise that while I never thought I was a homophobic person, I had laughed at jokes about gay people, laughed at the stereotypes on TV, never realising that I was giving a very powerful message to my son. I was, in effect, laughing at him.

I think that because I was able to tell my son that I loved him JUST THE WAY HE WAS, and because I was able to have an open mind and ask questions of him and show him that I wanted to understand and that I accepted completely that being gay is inherent, not a choice, we developed a far richer, more honest and equal relationship than we would if he were the typical straight son.

I was there when he was born and there when he died. In between we had a funny old ride at times, but we learned so much about ourselves and each other that I have to say that I'm glad I had the opportunity to share some of his life. I'm the better for it, and in a strange way my son's death gave me a new life. I had retired to the country for a quiet life of painting, reading and fishing, but instead I now co-ordinate a support group of people for parents of gay kids, and get to speak to all sorts of groups of people about having a gay child and informing people about HIV/AIDS and how we coped with that. I think he is quite proud of me.

I was introduced recently on radio as 'a gay activist'. At first I felt quite strange about that and thought, No, I'm just a mum. But then I thought, Hang on, you are, you talk to people about your gay son and sometimes you get them to understand, and at least you make them think about it, so you are, you're a gay rights activist. And I feel good about that.

My dream is that one day being gay will be accepted and supported by all in the community, or at least the majority of people, so that gay people never have to be afraid or rejected or suffer any discrimination.

Most hepful books:
  *Beyond Acceptance*
  *The Family Heart*
  *Now That You Know*

*Written by a mother of two from rural Western Australia. She has parented two sons whose sexuality was accepted right through their teenage years so that there was no need for anyone to come out.*

*It is her wish that families, friends and society will learn to accept everyone as they are and will not humiliate and oppress anyone because of their sex, race, disability, colour or religion. 'We are all different from one another and who says my difference is better or more honourable than yours!'*

I was of the era when 'nice' girls did shorthand typing, then you met a 'good' man, got married and had children.

At twenty I had my first child and at 24 my second child.

I grew up in a Christian family. I had a difficult childhood with an extremely authoritarian father and a very passive mother. I was never accepted for who I was and my personality was always labelled as wilful and disobedient. There was no joy, acceptance or encouragement.

I knew that this didn't have to be what childhood and growing up was about. So I pledged to myself that when I had children, they would be shown love and respect. Their spirit and eagerness to learn about life would be nurtured and treasured.

I also knew that there had to be a sense of partnership in this relationship. There would be times when I would have to set 'boundaries' that my children might see as unfair or unreasonable, but I believed that with the right approach these difficult times could be negotiated successfully.

In other words, I wanted the best for my children. The irony is that I'm sure my parents wanted the best for me. So what do we really mean when we say we want the best for our children?

I believe all children need to be loved, nurtured and respected. Each child is an individual. Different from anyone else.

This presents an enormous challenge to parents. Large doses of patience and understanding are required as we learn to respect and love what is different and unique in each of our children.

What is especially challenging is learning to drop our expectations of what we want our children to be and to accept them for what they are. Maybe we want them to be scholastically brilliant and they're not, or we want them to be musical and they're just not interested.

Supporting my children to be themselves often brought us into conflict with other people's expectations.

Both my sons had interests that ranged across the spectrum of sport, academia, music and theatre. They didn't think that being male should restrict or benefit them in these activities. They were both champion sportspeople and won scholarships for their music and theatre interests.

My elder son, during his final year at primary school, decided that making pot holders was going to be more interesting than doing woodwork. When he expressed this view he was joined by other boys in the class who felt the same way. The teacher agreed. However, within days the teacher received letters from parents expressing concern that their sons were doing sewing and demanding that they do woodwork.

My younger son had a similar experience when he was about eight years old. Some of his girlfriends were doing jazz ballet and he thought it looked great. The teacher welcomed him joining the class and everyone was happy.

Within weeks, a number of his boyfriends decided it was a great idea as well and wanted to join the class. Mothers openly expressed to me their concern about sons doing jazz ballet and I know that a number of boys were forbidden from joining the class.

Nurturing the uniqueness of a child and loving the person who is emerging is an essential part of our parenting.

My parents had an image of what a daughter should be and how she should behave. They never stopped to value me for who I was. I did not fit their picture of the perfect daughter.

I am aware that I did not always acknowledge my children's differences and I sometimes had expectations that were unrealistic and probably unfair. I tried really hard though to remember that my children were dependent on me to guide them and that this was an awesome responsibility. At times it would have been easy for me to use my power as an adult to dominate them and even frighten them into obeying me.

The bottom line surely is that as adults we want to be loved, respected for our opinions and listened to. We want to be valued. So do our children.

My work and lifestyle meant that my sons were exposed to a wide variety of people, opinions and values. They learned to question, seek answers and develop their own views on whatever challenged them.

When it came to sexuality I practised the same tolerance, acceptance and respect that I had used throughout their rearing.

Both sons had numerous male and female friends and were popular and accomplished in sport, music and their academic pursuits.

Both boys struggled as we all do through those years of puberty when we try to understand and enjoy our hormonal changes! It is an exciting time but it's often quite confusing. Lots of peer pressure, media influence and expectations from everyone around us.

I watched with pride, anticipation and some anxiety as my sons became men. These were the same feelings I'd had as I watched them deal with their schoolwork, achieve in their sporting careers and follow their interests in music and theatre.

One son is heterosexual and one is homosexual.

As I said, I wanted the best for my children. In other words, they must be nurtured and loved for who they are and encouraged to develop their spirit in the way that is right for them. Not what is best for someone else.

So whatever their sexuality, I want what is best for them and I apply those principles of love, nurturing, acceptance and respect that I consider so important for myself and for everyone else.

My husband and I are proud of both these beautiful young men. We have made wonderful friends with their girlfriends and boyfriends and have been enriched by the variety of people who have come into our lives.

We have anxieties as well as great joy as we watch these young men pursue their careers, make life choices and contribute to society.

*Written by 59-year-old Terry Stewart from Waikanae, New Zealand. Terry is the author of* Invisible Families *and she and her husband, Ron, are now retired. They have been married for 31 years. Terry worked for ten years as a Magistrate's Court clerk, then spent eighteen years at home raising two sons. In her late forties she completed tertiary certificates in areas concerning mental health, community education and journalism.*

As parents we may unwittingly internalise or assume strong heterosexual expectation for our children. When our child seems to be seriously going against our own moral, ethical or legal standards we may become fearful, or temporarily panic. I am pleased to contribute to this book and share our experience, for as a family we have 'been there, done that'!

Our story, with those of other New Zealand families, resulted in the writing of my resource book, *Invisible Families*, first published in 1993 and updated in 1996 by Tandem Press—four years after discovering, to our surprise, that our elder son happens to be gay. It is only his love, courage and integrity which allowed me to write this book. We are very proud of him.

My research shows that many homosexual people may realise from even five or six years of age that they are 'different' but do not know 'why' until they are older, some not until they are in their twenties. Others may marry, only to have a sad awakening. Our son was sixteen years old when he knew the interest in girls he was expecting to experience was not going to happen, and slowly recognition came that he was gay. He went to boarding school in his final school year and confided in his peer group, who then gave him an extremely rough time.

At this point we had no idea of his distress for he hid it from us deliberately. As he later explained, 'Those dearest and nearest are often the last to know because friends are dispensable but your family is not.' After gaining university entrance he decided not to go, found work, left it, went apple-picking around the country, and finally took off to Australia while still not quite eighteen years old. He had the money and we could not stop him. We knew something was very wrong but he refused all attempts to help him.

There followed four years of difficult communication and undeserved but out-of-character treatment, during which we suspected everything except homosexuality. Back home three years later it was not much better. Having no car, he boarded in town and met a young man who became his partner for the next five years. When their landlady remarried they had to find other accommodation. Still not 'out' as being gay, they came home to board. We hoped this would restore our once excellent rapport with our son.

One day I went into their room to find that their two mattresses were side by side in the middle of the floor. I called my husband in and we just KNEW what was the cause of all his and our heartache. We watched them carefully but they never gave themselves away by even a glance. When they made plans to move away I eventually summoned up the courage to ask if this was a relationship. After they consulted, he said yes, it was!

Initially we felt an enormous relief—here was an explanation for our anxiety. I asked if he had been molested or abused when younger, and he assured us he had not. Over an hour, he told us what had happened to him. We hugged and shed a few tears. Loved and accepted, he thought that was that, but for us came fear for them. The panic, confusion, imposed guilt and questions crowded in. Off they went, in love, leaving us in a turmoil.

We were out of our depth. What would his life be? Would he be lonely? Contract AIDS? Suffer from intolerance at work or on the streets? How had this happened? Was our parenting at fault? Had he been seduced? Where to get trustworthy answers or advice? Who to ask or to tell? What of other family members? What of church attitudes? These fears are valid for those raised in a judgemental society.

To our horror we learned that due to accumulated stress our son had attempted suicide with pills given to help him sleep—the school thought he had exam nerves. In fact he was victimised and harassed so unmercifully that he dared not sleep. There were no openly homosexual groups or gay publications in those days. He approached a local church for help and was told to repent this 'perversion' and pray for the 'evil' to leave him. Later he had some hard experiences overseas and in despair had turned to street drugs for a while.

We were appalled. These facts shocked us deeply, much more than his homosexuality. In private we both cried over his hurt, feeling we had let him down by not being more aware of his needs, all the more so because he is academically bright, articulate and a high achiever with a strong character. It devastated us to see how deeply and quickly his earlier, strong self-esteem had collapsed.

At this point I was challenged to write my book. My husband was totally supportive. We learned together and the whole process was enriching, enlightening and extended all our boundaries. Other family stood by us. Not all of them understood the issues or the need to confront them, especially 'using your own name, dear', but I believe they soon saw it was 'love me, love my kid, so love my book'! Initially it was a true exercise in 'feel the fear and do it anyway'. Through the media I asked for people to contact me and fill in a questionnaire. This was my own 'coming out', the point of no return. Happily, I received over 300 replies.

The research led me into previously unthought-of topics. I met people from hitherto unknown walks of life and those living with HIV/AIDS; I rethought my church allegiances; and I learned to ask for help when out of my depth. I feared reprisals from the local community but received no abuse and only a few disagreeable letters.

We were mortified to recall that we had signed against the NZ Homosexual Law Reform Bill in 1986 (sadly our son knew this), not from malice but because, unthinkingly, as many people do, we believed what our church leaders were saying and did not question this information. And because, like many people, we mixed homosexuality with paedophilia. We regret this lack of personal responsibility very much.

I was completely unprepared, humbled and often shocked to read the letters and replies from all those who trusted me—a stranger—from their deep need to be heard. One lad was considering suicide, living in the country thinking he was a freak and alone. A lass signed herself 'animal Andrea'—she was rejected by her family. Another young lesbian was raped by a family member, to show her what 'normal' sex was and how she could enjoy it if she tried. A mother wanting to nurse her son with AIDS was told to choose between him or her marriage—she chose the divorce. These wonderful people bravely laid their lives, joys and hurts out there to the whole world and I honoured and loved each one of them.

I do realise it is hard for many heterosexual people to understand that their expectations of sexuality—that is, what is the 'norm' for themselves—is NOT right or a norm for homosexual persons. I came to see that for lesbian, gay or bisexual people, sexuality is an inclusive state of BEING. I'm not talking about BEHAVIOUR. Ask yourself, just when exactly did my sexuality develop? Can this be split off from my persona? Doesn't sexuality subconsciously colour my whole personality and most of my reactions?

To have good self-esteem and be gay or lesbian is not uncommon—of course many gay and lesbian people lead untraumatic and happy lives. Even so, the generalised public homophobia is a strain, and is undeserved. Contrary to upbeat exposure of gay parades when there is a focus on the more extrovert behaviour and glitzy cross-dressers, most homosexual people lead quiet lives, passing as straight in the community, and are law-abiding, tax-paying citizens. Many live in committed partnerships and own their own homes. The gay parades are a one-day-a-year statement of self-determination against the other 364 days of overwhelming heterosexuality in society. As long as participants stay within the laws, such parades are essentially no different from the heterosexual carnivals and fiestas worldwide.

The fear of homosexuality is called 'homophobia'. It arises from anxiety, embarrassment or poor information, particularly about certain behaviours, and through not being at ease with sexuality in general. The effects of homophobia are often very subtle but can and do result in harassment, assault and even rape by heterosexuals, besides overt discrimination in education, housing, employment, health, justice, churches and other areas.

It is easy for people to say, 'I have no prejudice against homosexuals: as long as they do not express their sexuality; are not visible; and it is not actually MY child.' There are constant put-downs, jokes or comments such as, 'What a pity they've spoilt the use of the word gay,' yet spoilage of such words as queen, fairy or faggot isn't such a problem! And what about words like poof, dyke, queer and so on—what about letting derogatory use of these pass without comment? There are several explanations as to how the word 'gay' became popular, the one I like best is that it is an acronym for 'good as you'.

We are deeply hurt as families when we hear our loving, law-abiding children thoughtlessly or deliberately denigrated. We are great keepers of secrets, fearing for their jobs or societal repercussions. Some parents had never before told anyone they had a homosexual child. Some dared not sign their letters because they lived in small communities and feared recognition. We feel sad that there may be no grandchildren. Yet today many couples are infertile and grandchildren are not assured from any relationship. Such things greatly affect our own self-esteem, and our daughters or sons can even be deeply homophobic themselves. Then they may live in a state of stressful duality, fearing to be themselves or come out in any way.

This is extremely detrimental to their mental health. Often, particularly in the past, this has led to unsustainable marriages, harmful, covert liaisons and great trauma for all concerned. When to be yourself meant your behaviour was deemed criminal or you were put into a mental asylum (often by your ashamed family), given dreadful shock treatments or aversion therapies, there were few options. The extroverts acted out, the introverts kept painful secrets, and the result was/is a cynical, often unhealthy ghettoising of the homosexual communities.

Another problem is the stereotyping. ALL gays are effeminate, sex-mad, neurotic, promiscuous, artistic or child seducers; ALL lesbians are man-haters, can't get a man, are butch or after little girls. In fact, homosexuality knows no boundaries of status, work, race or religion.

When our son told us he was gay, I wanted to know 'why' this happened to him. I found many other parents, like myself, feared they might have unknowingly 'caused' their child to be lesbian or gay. But if you read the list of 'reasons' given by parents as to why they felt this might be so—there wouldn't be a heterosexual child left! Psychiatrists and psychologists removed homosexuality from their manuals as an emotional or personality disorder just over twenty years ago, yet how the stigma lingers.

Many parents have no trouble accepting or understanding their lesbian or gay children's sexuality. Others do find it harder.

I found that although many parents initially reacted somewhat negatively, most, with TIME, support and good information, eventually came to a state of loving understanding. We accepted our son totally. We realised he knew his own self and was not being misled or rebellious. His father felt we had been adequate parents although he regretted not questioning our son more firmly when seeing him upset. As many parents do, I did a 'guilt trip', having assimilated misinformation from the 1960s which said THE FAMILY and particularly THE MOTHER were responsible for anything that was not 'normal' in their children.

At present, research has not produced definitive answers about homosexuality. When confused by research, we need to ask why it has been done, for what purposes and how it was done, and, particularly, WHO funded it. We need to be aware that anyone can write a paper or trade off 'authority' or claim research status. The latest research is now strongly indicating a genetic predisposition, together with 'in utero' and even later hormonal developmental factors and also that hormonal changes may cause fluidity in sexuality. Words such as 'chosen lifestyle' or 'preference' are not appropriate.

I strongly believe we cannot accept a person without accepting the behavioural expression of their sexuality. This is a right. Some people have strong sexual and loving needs, others can easily be celibate—same as heterosexuals. Could you, especially when younger, have been permanently celibate, say from tomorrow, forbidden by others to give or receive any sexual expressions or love until you died? Normally, do we not accept others for their personality and talents?

Some women are oriented as lesbian but others may have made a choice based on experience of male abuse, or sometimes because of a feminist perspective that means they feel safer and more comfortable with other women. As adults, this is their right within the guidelines of personal integrity and responsibility to others.

Some people fear that teenage 'conversion' to homosexual behaviour may occur if education acknowledges differing sexualities. Certainly many youngsters experience intense, same-gender friendships but I found that if they are given sound information they are well able to differentiate their feelings. Mainly teens need acceptance from their peer group, as they hate to be in any way different. Research, although sparse, shows peer experimentation not to have any lasting effect.

Of course, anyone traumatised into believing they are gay or lesbian when they are not, should seek well-informed PROFESSIONAL counselling if they wish to reassert their heterosexuality. This may be a traumatic process not easily accomplished.

Not all homosexual people are angels! They are no better and no worse than any of us. Nothing happens in some homosexual behaviour or venues that does not occur in heterosexual equivalents, and there are roughly 90 per cent more of us. Paedophiles (sexual abusers of children) are known to be 97 per cent male heterosexuals. In a recent study of 260 cases, only two perpetrators were found to be gay or bisexual, which means that a child is almost 100 per cent more likely to be abused by a heterosexual. It has been established that abuse is most likely to come from their mother's male partner, another family member or a friend rather than a stranger.

'Gender' refers to male, female or transsexual and not to 'sex', which as a word has multiple meanings. There are also specific differences between drag queens, transvestites and other cross-dressers, all of whom we need to remember are some parents' loved child. These terminologies are often mixed with a fine disregard for accuracy, confusing families and the public while feeding the manipulative behaviour of some religious groups and often, regrettably, the media.

Several people wrote to me sadly questioning whether God, who made them, still loved them. Many felt alienated from church denominations, not over matters of faith but from imposed guilt, fear and others' NEEDS to preserve the MAN-MADE church structures, doctrines and theologies.

Many scholars consider the Bible, especially the Old Testament, to be a strongly political document. Undeniably, the ancient kings had a vested interest in encouraging high levels of population growth to replace those slain in the savage wars constantly decimating their tribes. Many priests of the old religions were homosexual. What better way to establish your own power or new religious ideas than to eliminate the opposition with stern sanctions against homosexuality? Having no conception of genetics or brain chemistry, this outdated wisdom sought somehow to explain the inexplicable.

I cannot believe the vitality of the Spirit or Word of an almighty God is bound or restricted by such human limitations. I do recognise that not all churches or those within them engage in bigoted fundamentalism. Most of the mainstream churches have support groups for Christian gays and lesbians (which for many are a life-line), but personally I find this to be somewhat hypocritical and patronising. Isn't an individual's church membership (or ordination) to be based on their Christian commitment and integrity?

Another great sadness for me was for those who wrote of experiences relating to HIV/AIDS. Too many families have heard a son say, 'Mum, Dad. I'm gay and I have AIDS.' HIV is now spreading too fast in the worldwide heterosexual community and we must all be vigilant. To ignore this fact is to invite tragedy.

Some of you will know that the appalling number of attempted and contemplated suicides of our sons, daughters or friends is not a myth—it is real and horrendous. This is due to the adverse pressures from society and, regrettably, often within their birth family. In despair, they become careless of self and are at risk from eating disorders, abuse of drugs and alcohol or from predatory persons.

How does one define evil or perversion? Where do our homophobic attitudes come from?

Much of it has been laid down by earlier judgemental, misinformed religious dogma which has pervaded our laws and attitudes. Society is always threatened by and cruel to those seen not to conform. We must all be challenged as to our speech, attitudes or lack of action. Stereotyping is quickly picked up by the young around us. They in turn, not understanding, readily victimise any schoolmate seen or thought to be different. If we say, 'Oh, these homosexuals are awful and make me feel sick,' we ignore that our own neighbour or best friend may have a homosexual family member.

What can we do about it? I firmly believe part of the answer lies in anti-discrimination laws and in school health/sex programs which educate and build teenagers' self-esteem. Some parents are equal to the task of such education but many more are not. For the sake of the less fortunate young people, it is vital that government programs are implemented and given support by school boards, trustees, and parents.

At the beginning of my research I did not set out to prove a point. Had I uncovered proof that somehow as parents we had been, albeit unconsciously, a cause of our son's homosexuality, I would have been truthful. In some ways it would have been easier—we could have all gone off for counselling! Naturally, parents feel it would be safer and less difficult for all concerned if their children were heterosexual. This is not non-acceptance unless such feelings continually override our thoughts.

I ask people to challenge any prejudice, open their minds and seek updated information from a standpoint of love—the unconditional love of all humanity, which Christ stressed and prized the most highly. It is my dream today that soon parents will feel able to allow their lesbian and gay young people to investigate their sexuality from the shelter of home, as a right, like their heterosexual siblings—to flirt a little, to take time over love and commitment. To feel empowered to say 'no' or 'not yet' rather than fall into despair, flee to the cities or tumble headlong into any relationship which presents itself.

I am pleased to report that our son is a well-adjusted, happy young man living in a committed, loving relationship. He has an employer who values his abilities and work which challenges his potential. We love his partner as another son. It is now hard to look back and recall our earlier, misguided confusion and fears.

As families we may feel 'invisible' because, with good reason, we fear reprisals in society, the workplace and the churches towards our daughters and sons. This barrier becomes largely self-imposed. We need to keep a sense of perspective and above all NEVER stop loving and supporting our child. From a position of good information we have strength to take on the world. I encourage you to claim the respect which is rightfully yours, to 'walk tall' and no longer be afraid or 'invisible'.

Most helpful books:
   *Beyond Acceptance*
   *Loving Someone Gay*
   *Living in Sin? A Bishop Rethinks Sexuality*
   *A Separate Creation*

*Written by a mother of two from Adelaide. Her two daughters are both in their early twenties. She says, 'When I wrote this letter I expressed what I felt at the time, but that time has passed. My daughter and I have since forgiven each other. She shares her thoughts and accepts mine. We needed time, that's all. When I look at her these days I see a confident, loving, generous woman who is completely herself. As she always was. I love you, Stephanie.'*

Our photograph albums tell the true picture. My daughter is gay. I have cried over every one of those pictures that show how little I saw for nineteen years.

There's the photo taken on the second birthday of my beautiful daughter, Stephanie, wearing a flower-printed dress. Her long, curly chestnut hair streams down her back and her face is lit up with her adorably mischievous smile. Even as a chubby infant, she had enough character to make a photograph into a statement about her personality.

After this we have the kindergarten photos where 'Superman' tied an old blanket marked with a big 'S' around her neck, and wore overalls or shorts. Anyone who had the temerity to say, 'What a beautiful girl,' was given a glance of scorn, raised eyebrows, and a distinct, 'I'm a boy.'

Year after year, there are records of family Christmases, but until I glanced through the album recently, I didn't realise that I never won the battle of getting her into a dress. Other than when wearing school uniform, she is wearing boys' clothes in every photo.

As she grew older, she refused to go to the school dances unless 'fancy dress' could be worn. My Steph couldn't be coaxed into girlie frills, satin or sequins. She went as Robin Hood or a river boat gambler, as two of our later photographs testify, and looked the handsomest 'boy' in the room.

On almost every page in the albums, there's a picture of her in the centre front of a sporting team. Although not always the best player, she was invariably chosen as captain. She could combine disparate individuals and form a team. Our photos prove that from her first boyfriend to her last, no male ever wanted to give her up. They brought their following girlfriends around to meet her, and when she showed no jealousy, they brought groups of boys instead. She used the cover of 'tomboy' for years and it made her very popular with the opposite sex. I could see her attraction, her naturalness, and admired her for not playing the very female game of flouncing around, manipulating males. This, I thought, was the first step in equality, treating males to honesty rather than techniques as her sister did with such talent.

Two years ago I had no worries. I had produced a well-balanced and lovely daughter, not only very beautiful, but with a generosity of nature few could resist. I took the credit for her irresistible sense of humour and her quick understanding of the ridiculous, as I did for every one of her assets. Her artistic talents, her paintings, her designs, the stories she has written and her sporting achievements filled me with pride back then. Then. Before she admitted to homosexuality.

Although I took the blame, I felt completely betrayed, by my family, by my genes and by my own upbringing. I tried to pretend I didn't care and I clenched my jaw firmly against criticism. For a while I let my husband think that his fault was as great as mine, but I knew deep down, since I have a gay brother and a gay cousin, that my daughter's homosexuality had been passed on genetically through me. My guilt made me feel suicidal and at times murderous. I couldn't come to terms with ruining the person I loved most in the world. It seemed that no matter how hard I scratched my way through life, I would never make it bleed the way I bled. I turned off my emotions by day and let them wet the pillow every night.

Since I ruined my daughter, I saw that somehow I had to fix her, and so I soaked up every bit of information I could find on homosexuality. In the process, I discovered that those, and there are a few, who think that homosexuality is passed on genetically through the mother have a very slim case. Logically, bearing in mind that a mother can only pass on a female X gene to her daughter, the premise is errant nonsense.

The next premise, influence, reared its ugly head. Many times I told my daughter that girls were as good as boys and could accomplish far more. Of course I did. I had my children in the early seventies when books for first graders that depicted stereotypical jobs for males and females were frowned on. But neither of my daughters played with dolls. Both preferred Lego, jigsaw puzzles, books, and inventing games rather than watching television. If this caused one daughter to be gay, it should have had the same effect on the other.

But I still had to punish myself. Because when I looked deep down, I realised that I had treated my daughters differently, in a very basic way. I had given Stephanie more physical love than her older sister, who never seemed to like me much. My baby was cuddlier and never turned her head away from my kisses. I can't remember ever smacking her. This I put down to the fact that she listened to me and then went off, considered the issue and made an informed decision. An admirable quality, I thought, so different from mine and so very opposite to her sister. Consequently, there's no photo of her sulking or crying.

After two years of self-flagellation, I realised that I couldn't take responsibility for her sexuality any more than I could for her leadership skills. Both were her individual qualities, instinctive rather than learned. From there, I worked out that I can't take the credit or blame for anything she is or does, and she is and does many wonderful things.

I can look through the albums now and see what I thought I had, but I can also see what I truly had: two daughters, individuals who grew up to be their own illusions, not mine. Two people who didn't really belong to me from the moment they were born. Reality. That 'tomboy' in her first cricket team, with her long hair hidden under her cap, didn't laugh with delight while the boys on the team she captained told the opposing team that a girl had bowled them out. She smiled to hide the hurt of being only a girl.

Looking at our photograph albums, I now see that I never understood her or what her every outfit tried to tell me. I feel insensitive because I didn't recognise her homosexuality, and hopeless because now that I do, I want to change it. I feel selfish because I don't want her to be what she is. It seems like a betrayal of womanhood—to me worse than a death—because she's still here, but not really here. The sparkle has gone, the mischief, the smile. All we have left are insincerities now that she's discovered she's gay. Perhaps that's what we always had, because of my denials.

Recently, her father and I invited her to dinner in a restaurant and made it quite clear that we'd like to meet her partner, from whom we'd been kept hidden. She turned up looking absolutely stunning and with an old boyfriend. With no other choice, we imitated a normal family for three hours until she left. After that, I cried for two days. I'd been given her idea of my stereotype again.

We can't survive with this lack of communication. I now question the love I have for my daughter, who once could not have been cruel to anyone. Not giving me a chance to face reality is a huge slap in the face and a statement about her lack of faith in me. I don't doubt that her adolescent behaviour will pass, but I'm terrified that whenever I have to insulate my heart, a tiny piece dies.

The hardest-hit parent seems to be the same-sex parent. Perhaps to the other it's a compliment, I don't know. The only thing I expected to pass on to my daughters at birth was my sexuality, not my colouring or my nose. Not passing on my essential being hurts. Eventually I'll accept it, but I haven't yet, nor has my daughter. I feel I can never be happy again.

Normally I lose myself in writing but the reality of this letter has taken me back to the world I can't cope with. I don't want reality. I want a new picture in my photograph album, my family back together again, both daughters with opposite-sex partners, full smiles, the fantasy world that I pictured since their births.

But I can't have it. That's the only true picture.

*Written by Pamela Du-Valle from Adelaide. Pamela said, 'At last I can put my finger on something tangible in regards to my son's nature and behaviour as he was growing up. It now all makes sense, why he didn't like to mix with other children, especially boys. He was frightened I would notice his attraction to them. I feel very sad that he experienced so much pain and confusion.'*

*Pamela's favourite quote is a powerful one: 'I would rather be hated for who I am than loved for what I am not!'*

The happiest day in my life was in September 1974, the day my only child, my son Ben, was born. As I held this little bundle of joy in my arms, a small human being, I had no idea how he would be at 21—I just knew he was a very special being. His birth was a dream and then a reality. I had tried for eight years to conceive, with two husbands. My son's father was my second husband.

My doctor had told me I would never be able to have children due to a medical condition (endometriosis), so I remember the incredible joy of holding my son for the first time. He was a miracle come true.

My life with Ben has been quite traumatic, with three failed marriages and no family to support me. I brought him up on my own and life was quite a struggle. Due to my own low self-esteem, I was quite promiscuous and had many traumatic experiences with men, but I always took great care of my son. He had learning difficulties and has a heart condition, so I was always seeking help for his learning problems and his medical conditions, which include bad coordination. I tried everywhere to get him help.

From about eighteen months of age, I noticed a different pattern emerging. Ben didn't like playing with other children, male or female. He didn't like the usual toys for boys, like trucks, trains, blocks etc., yet he was given all the boyish toys. He would throw them away and loved playing with an old wig of mine, leaves off the tree, dressing up and carrying Miss Piggy around. This behaviour continued right through his life. He was fascinated with horror and 'Star Trek'.

Ben didn't have any schoolfriends—he was a loner and spent hours inventing stories and drawing on his own. He spent weekends with his biological father and weekdays with myself, so a lot of his unusual behaviour was put down to him having a dysfunctional family, and being torn between two very different parents, with different beliefs and values.

As he was growing up, if I heard any bad remarks about

homosexuality I would always say, 'You should never say that, as you don't know how your children or grandchildren will turn out.' I have never been a racist or had any prejudices against creed, colour, religion or sexuality. Yet I came from a bigoted religious family with a very abusive stepfather and an angry mother, and I was much mistreated and abused as a child.

So why I had this innate intuitiveness about gays while my son was growing up, I don't know. My son mentioned to me when he was fifteen that he thought he was gay. He cried and I just held him in my arms and told him I loved him. He then went to live with his father, where he still is now, at 21. Ben never mentioned homosexuality to me again and I just thought, Oh, it's just a phase, and part of me hoped it was, yet another part of me knew he was different, and to be different is to be unique. To be fully human is to be different.

Five and a bit years passed and Ben and his father were not getting on so I found a therapist for Ben as he suffers from social phobia and panic attacks, and because of his heart condition he is unable to do lots of things, like drive a car, that other young people can do. Playing sport didn't interest him. After about six weeks of therapy he was able to tell me he was gay. This time I knew it was for sure and it was a relief.

I will always remember that day. It was a Sunday and he told me over the phone. 'Mum, I am gay.' I froze yet contained my voice and said, 'That's OK son, I always thought so and I am glad you have acknowledged it.' This was March 1994 and I was going to a rock concert that evening with a friend. I can't remember the concert as I was in such a daze.

Well, the sense of relief in Ben's voice was wonderful, but then he said, 'How do I tell my dad?' I said, 'Let's leave that till later,' and later we did tell him. I put down the phone and I was in shock—dazed and dissociated because my fears had been confirmed, and I knew it was true. What do I do now? Who do I tell? Questions, questions!

So I spent two weeks crying. I withdrew from life—who could I talk to, how do I handle this, will my friends accept myself and Ben? I cried for not having any grandchildren. I grieved for that loss. I questioned my own sexuality and my parenting skills. Was I a good mother? Did I cause this? All unanswered questions.

I had no extended family, just Ben and myself. It was like I went into the closet as my son came out. He blossomed and began going to Second Storey Hyde Out in Adelaide, a drop-in centre for gay young people. He started to make friends for the first time in his life. He had people who understood and cared. He shone.

He told his father in an argument and his father came to me and I had to confirm that our son is gay. His father is homophobic and does not mention it much at all, like it doesn't exist. My son chooses to stay with him for economical reasons. I finally made numerous phone calls to try to get some support for myself. I phoned Gayline and eventually found a mothers of gay children group in Adelaide. I began to read books and articles and had all my questions answered. Wow, what a relief.

It's easy for parents to think only of the bedroom and not the other part of a gay child's life. I soon learned a lot about homosexuality and have found that a great new life has opened up to me. I mix regularly with my son's friends. Some of these young people have no parents or have been kicked out of home due to having homophobic parents. It's so sad.

I have accepted my son's gayness and as a mother, I just hope he has a happy, long, fulfilling relationship with a stable partner when it is time for him to settle down. Right now, Ben is experiencing the social life most young people do at fourteen and fifteen, so there is plenty of time. He is making up for lost time and his loss of a free childhood.

I have recently remarried, for the fourth time, and my new husband and his family have accepted Ben and love and support him. Ben now has a real sense of family, with a new stepdad who loves him and accepts him and two stepsisters who love and support him. They even go raging with him too. I now have two step-grandsons who I adore—they are the grandchildren I thought I would never have.

My son has opened up a new life for Harry and myself. I am very active in PFLAG and have been interviewed in the local paper and on radio. I have got great responses and support. My mission is to help other parents come to terms with their gay children, and to educate the community about homosexuality in any way or opportunity I get. I will not tolerate homophobic remarks from anyone and I soon let it be known they are not acceptable.

I personally believe homosexuality is genetic and that it is just how it is. My son is still my son, a loving, gentle, sensitive young man. He is a human being and his sexuality does not make me love him less. In fact I love him more. As he once said, 'Mum, do you think I would choose to be gay in this hostile society? I wished I wasn't, but I am. I have to be real, this is who I am.'

I am glad my son is being honest in owning and honouring his sexuality. That is who he is. He is gay and he is now free. So I am proud, very proud of my son.

Most helpful books:
*Is it a Choice?*
*Beyond Acceptance*
*My Son Eric*

*Written by a mother from the central coast of New South Wales. She has been married to her second husband for nearly 22 years. She is a registered nurse and comes from what she considers is an ordinary, middle-class background. She is Catholic, but does not go to church.*

I married my son's father just after I finished my training as a nurse. I had my son at age 24. He was eleven weeks premature and quite a small kid for many years. I sometimes wonder if this had anything to do with his sexuality. I was to have four miscarriages to my second husband and decided almost fifteen years ago that perhaps God didn't want me to have any more children. I really regret that now, for when I go to the PFLAG meetings, the mothers that seem to cope better have other children.

I found out my son was gay ten days before his 26th birthday.

He didn't come out and tell me—I asked him. He didn't really say yes, but asked me, if he was, would it make a difference?

My son had a normal childhood and the only real concern I ever had was that he never seemed completely happy. I blamed myself for this as he was only five when I divorced his father, and I consequently spoilt him.

He was a very good athlete and left home at seventeen to pursue his chosen sport and complete his schooling. He never really lived at home after that. He got his degree and worked and lived in Sydney.

He was good looking and personable, with a great physique, and there had always been no shortage of girls. He had a serious relationship with a girl at twenty and would have married her, but she declined.

I had no reason to suspect he was gay, except that my husband a few months prior to the news, had sown a seed—he was dropping little hints. Unbeknown to me he had come home and told my husband five months before. My husband had told him he was not to tell me, as I wouldn't handle it—how right he was!

My first reaction was shock. I was numb and had an overwhelming feeling of sadness and loss. I spoke to my son about AIDS and sexually transmitted diseases and wanted to know if he was sure, or perhaps if it was a phase. He left before seven the next morning! Should he have stayed and discussed it more with both my husband and myself? I still don't know. No amount of talk, though, could have prepared me for my reactions.

I couldn't stop crying. I was nauseated and found I couldn't sleep. I was inconsolable, and even though my husband was wonderful, he couldn't help me. When I phoned my son it always ended in an argument, with me saying the most horrible things.

I nearly lost my job, as I was angry at everyone but unable to talk to anyone about it. A couple of weeks later I told two of my closest friends. One was wonderful, and the other—well, we have never had that old friendship since.

I was quite mad. I went through my son's room looking for evidence. I scoured the photo albums, trying to see if he 'looked' gay. I got rid of toys, books, sheets etc., everything I had kept for his wife and children. Throughout this time I had this terrible feeling of loss and sadness and the realisation that I had never really known my son. Worst of all, I wondered if it was my fault. Why hadn't my son told me years before? I couldn't believe my feelings—me a nurse who had seen so many things. I had always thought I was broad-minded!

Strangely enough, my Catholic religion never bothered me. I feel God loves everyone and I don't believe homosexuality is a choice. I think my son was born that way and it isn't his fault.

After a few weeks and numerous phone calls looking for a support group, I came across PFLAG. Heather sent me literature and that was an eye-opener. A month later I went to my first meeting.

The meetings helped us, my husband and I, because we were talking to people in a similar situation, but I needed more. I needed to know that someone, somewhere, had reacted like I had. I was jealous of some of the parents because they appeared to have accepted it quite well and I knew I hadn't. I felt my reactions had distanced my son even more, and because of the way I was, my husband was at a loss and blaming my son.

I found the help I needed some months later in a book called *Beyond Acceptance*. Some of the parents had reacted as I had—they had written down how I felt, and yet with time they were coming to grips with it.

It is nearly two years now and I cope, although I will always feel sad. I will never have grandchildren, and with my family and friends always have to keep up a pretence (my son doesn't want them to know). I worry that when I die, my son will have no one. It seems that most homosexual relationships are not long-lasting. He lives interstate now and has a partner, although up to now I haven't wanted to meet him. The reason? I feel embarrassed. I don't know why but I don't like to think of my son living close to another man. I worry about AIDS and also homophobic people. My son isn't bad because of his sexual preference. I don't believe society will ever completely accept homosexuality. I am more aware today of the derogatory remarks by young and old alike, and hate myself when I don't stand up—perhaps this will come with time.

At first I used to pray to God to change him, I don't do that now. Now I pray to keep him 'AIDS free' and help him lead a happy life.

I love my son dearly but still, God forbid, wish he was 'normal'. I hate myself for that and hope my son doesn't realise. I want him to know I love him and that I'm here for him—'God Help Me.'

Most helpful book:
*Beyond Acceptance*

*Written by a mother from Melbourne who was brought up in a Catholic environment. She and her husband have been married for 33 years and have five children. The youngest two are gay. Her advice to other parents is, 'Take one day at a time. Still keep loving your children as before and let them know they are well loved.'*

My 24-year-old daughter told us on Mother's Day in 1994 that she was gay. What a Mother's Day present. We had no idea that our daughter was gay so we were shocked, surprised, shamed and felt generally sick. We have met male and female gay friends of our children and were quite happy with them as people, but when it was our own daughter, it was a completely different story. We told her we loved her and gave her a hug when she told us, but I wanted to be sick and to faint at the same time.

I am Catholic and my husband has no religion. Our five children have been brought up Catholic. Our daughter does seem happier now that she has told her family. One sister, seventeen months later, is still finding it hard to cope with.

Our twenty-year-old son told us on 6 October 1995 that he is gay. Again shock, complete surprise for the family, hurt, guilt etc. The sister who can't cope with her sister being gay doesn't seem to be having any trouble with her brother being gay. After seventeen months of knowing our daughter was gay, we had told our close friends and had accepted our daughter as gay and were getting on with our lives. Now we are back in the mourning

101

stage. My husband and I are both devastated. We are very close to our son, the youngest of five. He's a real 'homebody', who, when not at uni, spends all his time at home. He seems no different since he has told us, although he is busy studying for his exams.

I told my brother that my daughter was gay and he wanted to know what treatment I was getting for her and told me off because I wasn't getting any. He has come around to accepting her now. Haven't told him about our son as it is only early days yet. We have only known for three weeks.

As it is the early stage with our son, I feel dreadfully alone, frightened of what people will think with two gay children. I find the books depressing to read as they are for parents with one gay child and some of them have taken five or eight years to come to terms with it. Mothers missing their sons who have died from AIDS. I wonder if I have all this before me.

Neither of my gay children has wanted to commit suicide. My son does not have a partner yet, as he is busy with his study. We are pleased that both of our children have been able to come out to us. We would rather know than not know.

We still love our children just as much and try to give them more hugs than before. Both children are kind, thoughtful and do a lot of work in the community with various organisations.

My daughter's gay friends are normal, friendly people. My son has not made any gay friends yet. I love both my gay children, but cannot accept the sexual act of one male to another. I am willing to read and learn how to try and accept. My husband and I are in a loving sexual relationship and the act of two males goes against all I have been taught.

My daughter went to the Sydney Mardi Gras this year. I find that the Mardi Gras as seen on TV does not do anything to help the image of gays. Men in brief underpants dancing around on the floats put friends of mine, and myself, off gays.

I feel sad and lonely for my children. My daughter has dropped most of her original friends and has made new friends through the gay outlets. Her boss knows she is gay and she has not been sacked, so that is a relief.

Reading other books has been a help to me, knowing the stages I am going through and what other parents have gone through, even the stage of thinking I could cope with my child having cancer better than being gay. This was a relief to read that other mothers had dreadful thoughts like this. I thought that with my first gay child, but am not thinking it this time.

February 1997. It is now sixteen months since our second child told us he is gay. He has recently told me that prior to coming out to the family, he strongly contemplated committing suicide. Parents need to be aware of the emotional strain their gay child is undergoing during the coming out process. We have always been very open with our children and I was pleased he was able to discuss with me his thoughts on wanting to commit suicide.

Most helpful books:
    *Coming Out*
    *Loving Someone Gay*

*Written by a 60-year-old mother of seven from rural New South Wales. She has been a practising Catholic all of her life. She says, 'With that comes a sense of loving others as God loves me. I especially see God in the wonders of creation.' She and her husband have reared seven sons, who they love very much. The family also includes four daughters-in-law, one fiancée, one partner and thirteen grandchildren.*

Homosexuality and tolerance—how do they touch your life? I'd like to share with you some of my thoughts and experience.

I am a woman in my late fifties, married for nearly 40 years, mother of several children. Twelve months ago, one of our sons told us he was gay. For some years we had wondered, but never voiced our thoughts to him, so in one sense his declaration was not unexpected.

However, thinking something and hearing it become fact are quite different experiences. We thought we handled it well, but next morning my husband and I looked at each other and burst into tears. Then came the task of accepting the situation, and for me this involved a 360-degree turnaround in thoughts, attitudes and words.

My previous attitude to homosexuality was generally one of ignorance, rejection and disgust—'these are sick people', it's an unacceptable perversion, an unnaturalness condemned by the church, and 'I sincerely hope none of them ever crosses my path' etc., etc. I couldn't begin to understand it, and I didn't really want to know, so it was a 'them and me' situation, and 'they' were wrong. As for HIV/AIDS, well, if you behaved as 'they' did, then it was your own fault if you got it.

However, twelve months ago, all this had to change. You see, I love my son very much, and there was no way that I could reject him, so this meant that a lot of things in me had to change, and I had to experience a new approach.

In this situation with my son, I had to train my mind and my heart to receive, perceive and understand in a whole new way. I won't pretend it was easy, and I am still in the learning process. The awareness that emerged most strongly at the time was this: I love my son very much. He is a wonderful young man, intelligent, loving and caring, creative, musical, very gifted in many ways, friendly, good looking, thinks for himself etc. Whoever he is, and however he is, he is the fruit of my body. My husband and I created him. I carried him within me for nine months and gave birth to him. Who he is, is the result of the genetic structure we passed on to him. I believe that totally. He was always different from the others, I knew that, and I know that his gayness was within him from the beginning of his life and not something he absorbed, or decided to try, or that society or circumstances have imposed on him.

At the time he first spoke to us, he was not, and had not been, in a relationship, so there was that initial sense of 'he's safe', but I would be lying if I denied the ever-present awareness of the risk of HIV/AIDS, and the fear that comes from knowing that many people in today's society are as I was, condemning and totally rejecting those who are gay, and therefore unacceptably different.

Would he experience rejection and humiliation? Would he be attacked, bashed up, perhaps seriously injured? The mothering instinct, the desire to protect and safeguard, remains ever strong.

However, I knew my son had to lead his own life, and that I had to stand back and allow him to do it, even though I sometimes feel very helpless.

At the time he came out, he chose to tell each member of his immediate family himself, which wouldn't have been easy. They accepted his news, though for some it was a struggle, and the ties of love and family remain strong. He is ours and we love him.

He is now in a relationship, and he and his partner have been home for a number of visits, including Christmas, with lots of family around. I really like his friend—a pleasant, caring, friendly young man.

I hear their terms of endearment, I occasionally see the loving gestures, as with any couple—a touch of hands, a look, a smile. I am aware of their care of and concern for each other.

It is still somewhat strange to me—I admit that—but I know that my love for my son will enable me to overcome this.

My experience of the homosexual community is quite limited, but those I know are warm, loving, friendly people. I'm not pretending for one minute that I've got my act together, or that I know what it's all about. Nor am I trying to foist anything on to anyone who reads what I am trying to say.

I do know that having the issue of homosexuality enter my life so personally has forced me to examine myself, how I feel and think, how I respond, how I go on from this moment.

Without that personal experience, I know that I would be taking much longer to reach this point.

This is only one area of my life where I have had to experience change, and I know there are many others. Because they haven't confronted me on a personal level, so far, I have sidestepped facing them. I am often intolerant of what I do not know, or understand, yet I am called, by God's love and acceptance of me, to be loving and accepting of the differences that are in each of us, just as I ask you to accept me, with all my funny ways.

Hopefully each of us can choose to reach out and grow.

I continue to experience concern for my gay son's well-being, but then, I have concern for all members of my family. When I am speaking of my family to others I often mention my son's gayness in an effort to convey to them my acceptance of his situation and perhaps to encourage them to think more deeply of their own attitudes.

*Written by a mother from Melbourne, who emigrated to Australia from Europe as a young bride in the 1950s. She and her husband have three adult children. Several months after writing the letter this mother relayed, 'The dire consequences I was envisaging at the time I wrote the letter have so far not eventuated, and if they do, together, I am sure we will find a way to cope. I am also quite proud of Lara's heterosexual friends for continuing to love her the way she is.'*

Our 25-year-old daughter came out to us four months before her departure to Europe. To fully appreciate the impact, I want to set the scene: my husband and I had just returned suntanned from a four-week backpacking trip to Far North Queensland. Brimming with tales and once again full of enthusiasm for youth-hostelling, we were looking forward to sharing our wonderful experience with the family. Our contentment came to an abrupt end.

On the fateful evening, shortly after our homecoming, almost exactly a year ago now, Lara had dinner with us. She looked radiant. Gone was the stressed expression on a pimply face, gone the melancholy, forlorn person she had presented two or three months prior to our departure. It was pleasing to see her bubbly personality restored to its former self. I couldn't contain myself any longer. We had always shared a wonderful friendship. 'And how is your lovelife?' I asked.

'I am seeing someone,' she replied. Happy for her, I eagerly enquired: 'How old is he? When are we going to meet him?'

'It's a bit more complicated than that,' Lara responded. 'It's a woman and she is 29 years old.'

My facial expression must have given me away. Lara walked over, hugged me with tears in her eyes. My immediate reaction was merely physical. An animal fear crept over my back, making my hair stand on end and my knees shake. I remember feeling old for the very first time in my life! We proceeded to the couch, sat down numbed and conversed about other things. 'It doesn't mean I'll cut my hair or lead a different lifestyle,' Lara hastily said.

'Where is the *Green Guide?*' was her father's reaction to the unwelcome announcement. Later we realised that this was his way of dealing with the situation. 'That's it? I knew you wouldn't throw me out, but . . .' This reaction was obviously not what Lara had expected. Having been in her first lesbian relationship no longer than two months, she had intended to come out to us that evening. I had made it easy for her.

Once Lara had left to return to the home she shared with her older brother, the scene in our house changed. We were in shock. How could this happen, why Lara? The question mark is still there now but not as intense.

Later that evening my tears began to flow. My diary, invaluable at that difficult time, reads: 'My world has collapsed! Why was she crying when she told us? When she confided in her brother, she was even howling. Is she crying out for help? He held her and said it's OK. We more or less gave her the same message.' Some days later I wrote: 'Not much more, apart from having a cripple, a terminally sick child or a dead child could have more consequences . . . could be more devastating.'

These were the words of a mother who had always considered herself beyond prejudice, who recently graduated with an arts degree in her mid–fifties and therefore has had much contact with young people. Furthermore, a mother who has during her studies completed a course on 'The History of Sexuality' and consequently is well-read on homosexuality. But this was no longer a case study or another theory—this has become the reality affecting my own family!

Steven, our 31-year-old son, has finally found his 'perfect partner' in Maureen. Our middle daughter lives happily with her family in Western Australia. Only our youngest daughter has been on her own for the last two years, busily coping with full-time teaching and the last semester of a part-time course at university. In her meagre spare time she plays soccer, and has done so 'to keep sane'. Now this! Up till now Lara has never been a source of any major worries. This is our very much loved and admired child who has grown into a confident young professional woman. She has been in two serious loving heterosexual relationships and has been the most traditional in outlook of our children. Lara has never given us any indication whatsoever during her life that her sexual preference could change. And she is the first to admit that these developments have taken her by surprise.

Lara considered herself 'straight', having been in close contact with many lesbians in her all-female soccer club. She certainly has been exposed to same-sex love for several years. Was she seduced—so lonely that she only felt half a person without being in a relationship? Is she experimenting? This would only be a phase, surely? Such were my thoughts before Lara left for her nine-month trip to explore her ancestry.

The resentment for her causing so much pain lasted several months. I would wake up and go to bed with the same dismal thoughts. Psychosomatic conditions surfaced and my menopausal symptoms recurred with a vengeance. The emotional support I needed was not forthcoming from my family, or only to a certain extent. The men were reticent, while I needed to talk. PFLAG did not seem to be of much help at the time either; only much later did I learn to appreciate their support. My case, my daughter's situation, was different, or so I believed!

At the early stage, considerable effort on my part went into persuading Lara to reconsider her relationship, particularly as she maintained, and still does, that it is her choice. I continually attempted to make her aware of the possible dire consequences to her personal and professional life, as well as ours. My fears for her future life were overpowering. Our friendship deteriorated, with Lara becoming defensive at my continued questioning about the future. On my troubled days I perceived Lara as lacking in judgement. But since when has love been rational! I saw her need to belong as a weakness. Most of her friends from the soccer club are lesbians, as mentioned earlier. In my opinion, she had finally given in, especially as she had told me previously that some girls had made advances towards her. Is she choosing to be a victim? Mind you, I am of European Jewish background and am very apprehensive of victimisation. Was history going to repeat itself, with a quirk?

During my positive periods, and they are much more frequent now, I can value her decision to lead a life of strong feminist convictions, a life filled with empathy and love. 'Mum, I am happy, it feels right, I am equal,' Lara assures me.

The lengthy entries in my diary reveal anguish and self-loathing. My belief that people basically do not change was shattered. I drew up lists of possible consequences, considered my own negative attributes and Lara's praiseworthy qualities. On re-reading this, I realise how uncomfortable we felt in each other's company for a while.

Being physically active helped me to overcome my perceived loss. Once more I went on regular early morning walks and continued with swimming and my own 'work-out' on a weekly basis. During my working hours my mind had to be on the education, health and safety of the young children in my care.

Coming out to one close friend of mine was not beneficial. I thought she would be the one to understand my pain. She was certainly familiar with suffering as her eldest son had been diagnosed with schizophrenia some time ago. I guess my 'problem' must have appeared infinitesimal in comparison to her torment.

I was grieving for the daughter I had previously known, for the loss of a special mother-daughter relationship. I was mourning for the grandchildren I shall never have and for their children's children. The future was going to be so different from my expectations. Perhaps I was even a bit jealous at times of the emotional closeness Lara would be experiencing in a lesbian relationship.

A sense of guilt crossed our minds only fleetingly. Hasn't Lara professed her sexual preference as her personal choice? From my reading of history I have come to the conclusion that a number of social forces are responsible for the shaping of sexuality. Our daughter has simply become part of a shift towards non-marital and non-heterosexual expression. But whatever our belief, our children are, as Jack Thompson declares, 'the sum of us'.

The real test of my acceptance will take place on Lara's imminent return from her travels. During her absence I believe I have made considerable progress towards enlightenment. Not only were we corresponding in a positive way, discussing the issue, but I initiated several meetings with her partner, Sophia, and enjoyed her company. By the way, Sophia had joined Lara for four glorious weeks in Europe and their relationship is blossoming, so I hear. I have yet to experience and feel comfortable in the presence of their demonstrative affections. I consider this a step towards approval.

Contemplating the period of twelve months since our knowledge of Lara's changed sexual preference, I rate time as the foremost healer. I learned the true meaning of unconditional parental love and the importance of the support and empathy of other parents with gay children. Other family members, to my shame, were much more quickly and freely accepting of this new situation. A willingness to recognise sexual diversity in my own children will surely pave the way for strong family ties in the future.

Most helpful book:
*Different Daughters*

*Written by a mother from Adelaide. She was born in the UK and came to Australia in 1966. She comes from a small family and has one older sister. She goes to church regularly and hopes that one day her young son will make her a grandmother.*

I was born in England and came out to Australia with my whole family. We came out by boat and stayed in Adelaide. My father could not settle so we travelled around for three years, but always came back to Adelaide.

My family values have always been 'work hard and long for money'. Money is very important. Not to spend and enjoy, but to keep on saving at all cost. I do not share the same values as my family. I am a believer in God and go to church but my boys do not.

We lived interstate when I was married and moved back to Adelaide after my divorce. My son Gordon, at Christmas 1994, came and sat on the kitchen bench top. When he had something to say to me he had the habit of doing this when I was cooking. He said, 'Mum, I am looking at an alternative lifestyle. I have been looking at my sexuality.' Gordon then told me he was gay.

When Gordon was in his early teens he had the habit of not eating his lunch at school but bringing it home and then leaving it in his bedroom. Every now and then I would go and look for it. I asked Gordon why he left it in his room. He said he was experimenting in growing penicillin. It was then I found books and video tapes. They were not of girls, but of men.

I sat down and cried. I did a lot of praying that my son was not gay. Then I put my head in the sand and hoped it would just go away. After Gordon had told me that he was gay I told him he was my son, he always would be, and I would never stop loving him. In the following months I have been trying very hard to come to terms with my son being gay. I have eaten for comfort and put on a lot of weight. I have done a lot of crying and at times have drunk too much.

I have to tell Gordon he must not tell any members of our family that he is gay. My father thinks that they are responsible for the AIDS virus and are the scum of the earth. I know my family would reject him and would try to make me do the same. I have told Gordon I will always stand by him.

After Gordon told me that he was gay I rang the Gay hotline to see if there was a support group for parents of gay children. The man I spoke to was very nice and helpful. He gave me the phone number for PFLAG. They only started up in Adelaide in September of 1994. Anyone can ring and go to their meetings for all the support they need.

I know I am very lucky to have the support that I have. The minister knows about Gordon at the church I go to and so does my home fellowship group, so there are many people around me to support me. When I first found out about Gordon I felt like I was the only person with a gay child and that I had no one to talk to.

I do not blame anyone for Gordon being gay. I believe he was born gay. Before, I did not know much about gay people. I am trying to get to know Gordon's world. Gordon has been beaten up just because he is gay.

I do not believe it is right the way gay people are treated. Some day they will be accepted in this world. God willing.

Most helpful books:
*The Church and the Homosexual*
*But Lord They're Gay*

*Written by Mollie Smith from Carlingford in Sydney. Mollie is a retired welfare worker who turned 71 in 1997. She and her husband, Ken, have four children. Mollie strongly believes that the myth of older people being rigid and unable to accept new ideas is untrue. She feels that her father shaped much of her outlook on life. He was an open, fair-minded man, with a well-developed sense of humour. Mollie believes PFLAG is an important organisation that opens windows, clears away cobwebs and educates parents to understand and accept their sons' or daughters' sexual orientation.*

We are a family of four—two sons and two daughters. Two of our children are gay, a son and a daughter, which makes for tidy statistics and good planning, some say!

It seems ages and ages now since we first learned of our two youngest children's homosexuality. My daughter was the first to come out, although she did not have much choice in the matter, since I asked her if she was a lesbian, which gave her a nasty shock at the time! Looking back, I don't think I chose the most opportune moment. We were on a shopping spree together and were having a meal in a Grace Brothers cafeteria. I had long suspected Liz was gay, and I could finally contain myself no longer. 'Liz, are you gay?' I asked across the spaghetti bolognaise. My poor daughter nearly choked, turning red and white in turn. 'Yes Mum,' she said and then we talked and I convinced Liz I was not going to make a big production of her lesbianism, and emphasised the fact that I loved her and accepted her as she was and I was sure the rest of our family would feel the same way.

Our son Peter handled his coming out himself. He approached us all in turn and we reassured him of our love and support. It was an emotional occasion and tears were shed. I felt very proud that our two straight children were able to easily accept and love and support their gay brother and sister.

But how did I feel? Relieved that we knew, that it was all out in the open. Concern for them as members of a minority group, for whom, despite many advances, there is still discrimination—sometimes overt, sometimes covert. Fear of them being violently assaulted, fear of HIV—every parent's nightmare. Fears they might be lonely.

The reality is that our son and daughter are well-rounded people with lots of friends, both straight and gay. They lead full and productive lives. Both of them are in stable and loving relationships. We feel they are both fortunate to have found people they love and trust, and the fact that their relationships are same-sex is irrelevant.

Like many parents, in the beginning of my long journey into learning about and understanding homosexuality, I had to work through many feelings. Guilt! Was it my fault, where had I gone wrong? What would extended family members think? Neighbours? Would they think we were a peculiar family? Some of these feelings were not very noble, but they were there and they had to be dealt with.

PFLAG helped. It was good to meet other parents, and to realise I was not alone. There were books to read, which helped a great deal. I have never experienced the depth of grief and sadness some parents suffer, but I still had my particular battles to fight. I feel, several years later, that I have grown as a person. I appreciate their qualities more than ever. We as a family love and respect them for the fine people they are.

I often feel very sad when I hear of parents who are unable to accept their child's sexual orientation. Some parents reach a certain stage when they say, 'I love you, but I don't want to talk about it.' Some parents refuse to meet their son's or daughter's partners. Others reject their children, casting them out of the family home, sometimes violently. To others, deep religious convictions are a barrier to acceptance, and they deny their children parental love and compassion.

I have long left behind my original reasons for joining a PFLAG group. I believe in KEEPING FAMILIES TOGETHER, and the way to do that is to provide support and education for parents and families. I always remind a parent that their son or daughter is still the same son or daughter they have always loved, and to remember they have bravely chosen to share their sexual orientation with their parents. Rejection is a very real fear for a son or daughter. Can we imagine how awful it must be to lose family support and love?

PFLAG has groups throughout Australia. In New South Wales we have a group meeting at Darlinghurst and now we have outer-suburban groups, at Parramatta and Campbelltown. These outer suburban groups are very important, because the population has grown rapidly in the western areas of Sydney, and there must be many parents, sons and daughters in these areas looking for support and information.

Our city and suburban groups receive much support from the gay community. In Parramatta and Campbelltown, ACON (AIDS Council of New South Wales) have been particularly helpful and supportive.

A particular feature of our meetings is the presence of gays and lesbians who come along to the group. Some of them come to prepare themselves for coming out to parents, and seek our help and advice. Others are there as support people, and they make a valuable contribution. For some parents, it is often the first time they have conversed with a gay person other than their son or daughter, and those conversations are often very emotionally charged, especially in the early days of coming out. I feel parents gain insights and understanding from listening to gay people talk of their experiences. When parents come out, very often they are self-centred, initially only able to cope with their own feelings, and this is when hurtful things can be said. I suppose for PFLAG the most difficult task is to become known. We have a high profile in the city, but in the suburbs there is still a lot of work to do to be recognised.

The Parramatta group, which I started in April 1995, is a case in point, where you know the need is there, but it comes down to making contact with people. We are growing and 1996 has seen an upsurge in membership. It is not an easy thing for parents to come along to a group, where they feel very vulnerable, unknown, and do not know what to expect. Several parents over the years have said to me that they felt very apprehensive about attending a PFLAG meeting and they were so relieved to find all the parents were ordinary people. What did they expect, I have often wondered?

In New South Wales we also have groups in the country, in Bathurst, Tamworth, Wagga Wagga. We also have a contact in Nowra and Newcastle.

Most helpful books:
*Invisible Families*
*Beyond Acceptance*

*Written by a recently retired father from rural Victoria who has lived most of his life in the one town. He has been involved with many organisations in the district. Happily married for almost 40 years, he has one son who is 36, and a 30-year-old daughter, along with two grandchildren. He has firmly-held Christian beliefs, and believes himself to be fortunate and happy.*

Our son had an amazing capacity to refrain from going to the toilet while attending primary and secondary schools in our country town in Victoria. We now know why—he was gay, and even as a child he felt uncomfortable with the boys in their toilet.

Ron was a fine-looking lad, polite, sensitive, industrious, very intelligent and loved dearly by his parents and liked and respected by his group of close friends. He had natural tennis ability at eight years of age but no competitive spirit or aggression. We would send him off to junior tennis on Saturday morning and he would enjoy himself with the other children, but on returning home he would be quite unaware of how many sets he had won. He appeared puzzled that we should think that beating his friends at sport was so important.

I will never forget his first real football match. He was selected to play with the local Scout cub team to compete with a team from a nearby town. I, the proud father, went along to the football ground to see my son represent his town. The ball came out to him, he ran quickly and picked it up skillfully. He then stood stock-still with the ball while, it seemed, the entire eighteen members of the opposing team jumped on top of him. I don't think that he went near the ball again. My dreams of a rugged footballing son ended that day.

Ron went off to Melbourne University and enjoyed a wonderful and successful first year exploring the wider world. His second year began not so happily. He rang home with a sob in his voice, explaining that the cause of his grief was that his bike had been stolen. We began to worry about his being so upset over such a small thing, and wondered how he was coping with life in general.

He graduated with honours and found a teaching position in a very good school. He soon became very immersed in a career which he loves, wrote several books and seemed very happy.

Our friends began asking us when Ron was going to get a girlfriend and get married. We had been quietly hoping for the same thing.

When he was about 25 years of age, our son came home for a visit and took his mother into the sunroom for a talk. He tried to tell her that he was gay by telling her that he would never marry and have children. He was so vague that his mother did not understand what he was trying to say. Then it was my turn for a talk, and I managed to work out what it was that he was so upset about.

Our Uniting Church Christian background had shown us that Christ had taught love and understanding for all—especially minority groups and the oppressed. We shared hugs and sent him back to Melbourne with the assurance that he was our son and that we would always love him. I am proud that Ron's sister has remained loving, understanding and fiercely loyal to him.

My wife and I spent many hours lying in bed at night discussing our son's problems. Many tears were shed for we really did not fully understand, and we so desperately wanted our son to be happy. It distressed me greatly that he had been so alone with his problem. As a youth, he had looked up homosexuality in our encyclopaedia to discover the truth about himself.

Time, as it does, has healed the hurt to a great extent and

hesitation when someone made a negative comment or told a joke concerned with homosexuality. But the reaction of other people was minimal. I had never suggested that the people I told should keep it a secret. But I always worked on the premise that it was not an issue that was appropriate to discuss. I didn't discuss the sex style of my heterosexual children, so why should I discuss the sex style of my lesbian children? In retrospect, it seems that this was a rationalisation for my closeted approach.

So, what has changed? I now talk about my lesbian daughters, particularly to people who I have not met for a long time. They say, 'Tell me about your children.' So I do. 'My son is in a long-term relationship with a woman. One of my daughters is married, with two young children. My other two daughters are lesbians, and one is a mother of a lovely teenage daughter.' It flows quite naturally.

I do not flaunt the lesbianism. So why am I writing this letter? This is surely flaunting the issue.

I am writing to all the parents of lesbians who are uncomfortable about their lesbian daughters. I am writing to tell you that your daughters are lesbians, and that is how it is. It is a lifestyle which is still condemned by many people in society. To be a lesbian is to be part of a minority group. And all minority groups suffer. Society is threatened by them. Society fears them. They are different, according to society.

But they are not different. They are women. They all have their individual differences. But they are living their lives their way. And it is difficult for them if society and also their beloved families treat them as if they are not normal. They are just as normal as all the rest of the people in the world. Who is normal, anyway?

The process of realising that my lesbian daughters are OK people has been a long one. It has been full of doubts, and disillusionments, and disappointments.

But in the final analysis, it saddens me that I have used up so much energy coming to terms with what is no longer, for me, an issue. Think about it . . .

*Posted anonymously from a mother in Sydney. To the writer of this letter, all I can say to you is that it hurts a lot to read about your pain. If you would ever like to talk confidentially, please don't hesitate to drop me a line. My address is on page 191 of this book.*

My son told me two years ago—eleven days after his 24th birthday—that he was gay. A pain shot straight through me, but I remained calm. If the truth be known, I suspected as much but had closed my eyes to it.

It did explain a lot about his growing-up years, though. He never seemed to fit in with his classmates and if he was invited to a party, or home to play with someone, he would want to go, but when the time came he wouldn't. He got to the second term in year nine and then wouldn't go to school. He ended up doing the rest of his schooling from year nine to year twelve by correspondence. I was afraid he would never be able to go out to work, but fortunately he got the job he wanted and is doing well at it.

He never made male friends at work, but has a lot of female friends, who all know about him and all seem to be very fond of him. These days he has a group of gay male friends and is living in a flat on his own.

From the day he told me I have never told a soul. I know if his father finds out he won't allow him to come home. I have told him that if he wants to tell his brother and sisters, he will have to do it, as I can't say the words. I think it is unnatural.

I know both his sisters suspect that he might be gay but find it hard to really believe it and haven't said anything to him. I'm sure they will both accept him. I'm not sure about his three brothers. They won't like it and I think one won't want to know him, and one will feel sick but will probably be all right in the end. The eldest one I am not sure about.

As for me, I still love him—he is my son. I am devastated, ashamed, worried, and while I realise people I know possibly already know, I feel that while I say nothing, nobody will say anything to me. Once it is in the open, I don't know if I can handle it.

I don't understand why people who are gay find it necessary to let the world know their sexual preference.

From the mother of a gay son.

P.S. I don't know if you are gay, I mean no offence to anyone. I just wish my son was not gay.

*Written by a mother from Perth.*

I was born in Western Australia. I grew up in the country until my teens, then lived in the city to finish my education. I trained as a nurse at Fremantle Hospital. I married a geologist in Kalgoorlie, where our four children were born. I guess I am a pragmatist and I am a firm believer that homosexuals are born and not made. With our son, we just accepted from birth that he was different and basically we just waited to see how the difference would manifest itself.

When he was in his teens, he and his brother obviously loathed each other and we had to keep them apart, literally—mainly in order for the rest of us to live in harmony.

Acceptance is a matter of intelligence, I feel, because if you had a child born with a missing limb or any physical disability, you accept your child and help it to cope with any difficulties in order to face life.

You see, my son didn't ever have to tell me he was homo-sexual and we have always been able to talk about all subjects. He has a high IQ and has told me he registered at puberty that he was different, but didn't know how. An enlightened teacher lecturing in human biology touched on differing sexuality and my son said it was like 'Saul on the road to Damascus'.

He had girlfriends in order to 'image' in his late teens, and that does help them to cope with their peers, because that is the hardest pressure to cope with. If they have to battle at home as well it must make life hell.

My son and his brother still don't get along, but his two sisters are very supportive and we all get along very well with his partner and all of their friends. One of the hardest things for us to accept was that he had to go away from home, due to archaic laws in our state. After getting his BA, he went to Melbourne to live and go to college to study writing.

He lives a happy life, when he is allowed to! Just recently he and his partner had their flat fire-bombed, and coming home from bars can be hazardous, but on the whole, he copes very well. Being six-foot-three helps, and he has confidence in himself, which I pride myself comes from his upbringing.

If you are an observant parent, you notice all sorts of things in your children when they are growing up and hopefully you can guide them where they need to go. Regardless of the adversity, all my children were taught to face up to it and sort something out.

Religion is not much help, that is the old registered religions, as they refuse to accept. One mustn't question anything. I have travelled a fair bit and have noticed that Caucasian societies seem to be the only ones that can't accept that homosexuality occurs.

I can't compare anything between my son and his father as my husband was killed in a mining accident fourteen years ago when my son was still at college. His father was accepting of his son, though he seemed to have a hard time grasping the concept of homosexuality, but we were able to talk freely at all times.

The hardest thing for me as a parent is seeing the hurt every day that my offspring has to cope with. The ignorance of his fellow man is mind-boggling, and how one educates them is beyond me. In a lot of instances it comes down to good old-fashioned manners, and they seem to have vanished long ago.

*Written by Bonnie Batzloff from Melbourne. Bonnie was born in Mareeba, North Queensland in 1934. Bonnie has worked hard all her life, often in manual labour positions, to provide for her family, and she worked for the Department of Social Security for twelve years, retiring*

*in 1995. Her marriage finished in 1982. She contributes spare time to PFLAG in an endeavour to help others.*

Eleven years ago my son told me he was gay. Although the idea had never occurred to me as a direct thought, I think I always knew. We are a very close family, my daughter, my son and I, and know each other well, so I guess it was not as hard for him to tell me as it may have been for some other people to broach the subject with their families. We've weathered many a storm in our years together and that has strengthened our love, friendship and support for each other beyond measure. Privately I shed a few tears for the tough times my son might face because of a few unenlightened people who might not see him for the person that he is, and see only the side of his nature which may challenge their prejudices and their ability to see past them.

My son told me that he wanted to mix more with people like himself and had found a gay sports association with which to play tennis. I had always known and welcomed my children's friends and told him I did not want that to change. A short while later he moved into a flat with two friends. He also introduced me to his boyfriend of the time. That was my first contact with his new community.

Next, I was invited to his birthday party. The reaction from the other guests was interesting, to say the least! Their looks said, 'Does she know?' and, 'How do we talk and act?' We were all so polite, it was stifling. Looking back now I have to laugh! It took a little while for them to relax and realise that I did know and that it was all right to be themselves. The same applied to me, getting over the awkwardness and uneasy little silences as we all moved toward a comfortable meeting point, which we did fairly quickly and painlessly. It turned out to be a lovely evening with good food, good music and lively conversation.

In time I became a sort of den mother, especially with the sports association. I went with my son to monthly meetings, sports days, swimming carnivals, theatres, brunches and dinners. At carnivals, I often started races and occasionally took part in games of captain ball, tunnel ball, and leader ball. I even bowled for a season with what was at that time the only gay bowling league in Australia. Then there was the annual ball on Queen's Birthday weekend when we went in costume and danced under the mirror ball. I've had a lot of fun with my extended family. When my son was overseas, I had no shortage of visitors and I was well-cared-for and kept involved with activities and outings. On Mother's Day that year my daughter and ten of the boys gave me a surprise brunch at a lovely little cafe, and presented me with earrings and a bunch of beautiful flowers. I've lived in Melbourne for six years now, yet whenever I visit Brisbane we manage to get together for a meal, a gossip and a bit of a laugh.

Being so closely involved in my son's activities brought me into contact with many of his friends and acquaintances, male and female. A lot of them talked to me on a very personal level, usually about their families' reaction to their sexuality—if indeed they had told their families. Some asked me whether I would meet their parents if their parents were willing, to which I always agreed. In six years I met only three mothers. In a lot of cases the sons' and daughters' sexuality had been fully accepted and they were living at home openly as themselves, as my son had, or had their own places and visited or wrote to their families regularly. Some had been rejected by all or some family members. I was surprised at how often it was a sibling who turned away. I found a lot of disappointment, sadness and hurt in varying stages of growth or repair. Very, very rarely have I met a person who did not want some contact with their family in spite of some extremely emotional confrontations.

How and when to tell is a major decision for a person to make. Some of the people who spoke to me had told their families while still living at home; others moved away and established a network of friends and supporters first. Others had no intention of telling—they saw no reason to do so. Most said they had realised at an early age that they were different from others of their sex and usually thought it was something they should keep to themselves. At some stage they discovered that they were attracted to people of the same sex or either sex to varying degrees. Schooldays were often pretty awful if their sexual nature was known or suspected. I read in the *Bulletin* magazine of 23 March 1995 of a report to the New South Wales government by the Gay and Lesbian Family Association which described instances of harassment of gay students, including a hanging with a school tie; a student being thrown onto a barbecue fire; and another being burned with a cigarette. I knew one young man who sought psychiatric help because he found his homosexuality so difficult to handle. It made no difference; he had to accept the way he was born.

Reasons for telling families varied, too. For some it represented the need for help, understanding, and reassurance that they were OK and loved for who they were. Others just wanted to stop pretending to be something they were not, whatever the consequences. Whatever time they chose, the telling was hardly ever easy. Some were able to plan what they'd say, where, and when; others got so nervous they simply blurted it out, sometimes in rather awkward situations. Having told, there was no going back, so they were more or less at the mercy of the moment, taking the risk of losing everything familiar. Telling doesn't always mean their troubles are behind them, especially for people still coming to terms with their sexuality. So often it is a case of giving emotional support to family members and helping them to come to terms with this new aspect of their child or sibling—a sort of reverse nurturing—while at the same time establishing their own whole identity in their own minds and lives.

There may be parents who blame themselves, thinking they have gone wrong somewhere along the way. Of course they haven't. I've been writing here about homosexual people I've met, and all said they were born the way they were—no choice. As one young man said to me, 'Why would anyone choose to be gay when it could be so much easier to survive in the straight world?' Then there are the families who don't want to believe or accept what they've heard, or hope it is a passing phase and will go away. Others, sadly, simply reject the reality and the person concerned. Each family's experience is its own and each copes in its own way. Thankfully, there are groups like PFLAG to help families and friends to realise that they are not alone; there are others who have been or are going along the same path.

It is not always easy to see that our son, daughter, brother or sister has not changed, only recognised a truth about themselves; we have not changed, only been presented with some new information that we need time to digest. Time is the main ingredient in balancing and accepting what cannot be changed. There will be things we may never understand or wish to know about but I don't believe there is a substitute for the open heart and open mind in keeping the bond strong between us.

Most of the homosexual people I know live quietly in the suburbs and have jobs, careers, studies or professions, just like any other member of society. My son is a public servant and his sexuality has not been an issue with his employers. His office makes use of his knowledge of gay community groups to target areas of need and information, and he has become a contact person for community service groups and social workers.

I'm often disappointed by the way the media portrays homosexual people. I've noticed in TV newscasts that whenever a story on gay issues is aired, pictures are shown of the most outrageously dressed and made-up people, usually in the Mardi Gras parade or similar setting. I wonder whether they are aware that Mardi Gras is actually a month-long festival with plays, concerts, art exhibitions and sports carnivals; the parade is the final event—a kind of fun closing ceremony. When we read about sports groups, for example, we are not automatically referred to smashed hotel rooms or airline passengers being harassed by teams of players off on an end-of-season trip. Neither example is typical of all homosexual people or sports groups. People are people first and foremost, regardless of race, religion, talent, interests, politics or any other facet of human make-up.

When I lived in Brisbane I was part of a support group for families, partners and friends of people living with HIV/AIDS, similar to the one in Melbourne which meets at the Positive Living Centre once a month. I was invited into that group by two enthusiastic social-work students on placement with the Queensland AIDS Council who saw the need for a meeting place where people could feel safe to share their experiences and gain support from caring people. As well as our two students and me, we had a retired nun, who was a tireless worker on behalf of people with HIV/AIDS, and had a delightful, saucy sense of humour. She was an inspiration and great support to all of us.

At that time, in the late eighties, there was still a lot to learn about HIV and HIV/AIDS, and there was a lot of misinformation and misunderstanding in the wider community, fostered, unfortunately, by a few scaremongers and homophobics in the media. There were still doctors who told patients who had tested positive to HIV that they could not hope for more than two years of life. Of course, we now know that not to be always the case; there are many vital, lively people who tested positive to HIV several years ago and remain healthy.

We met once a fortnight in a house donated for use as a medical and drop-in centre. Once in a while we had a guest speaker, usually a doctor or a counsellor, who kept us up to date with latest information on treatments, therapies and anything of interest to our group. It was very informal and open and of great value to all of us. We usually found on those evenings that the social workers, Sister and I were well and truly in the background as our group of parents and friends expressed their fears, asked questions and discussed sensitive issues with our guests, who were very frank and honest, which was just what was asked for—no pretty pictures or playing down of the situation. We all learned so much from these sessions—not just the information we got from the guests, but the kinds of issues that people really wanted to explore in the regular meetings. What they wanted above all was knowledge about the virus, what to expect, how best to help their loved one, how to cope with their own stresses.

It was particularly hard on parents whose sons had asked them not to reveal the nature of their illness to anyone else, not even other family members, apart from our group; they had the added burden of keeping the secret while their sons were alive, and having to deal with hurt, sometimes angry families when they had died. I've met brothers and sisters who were terribly upset because they had been denied the opportunity to accept their brother's sexual nature and illness, and the chance to say a loving goodbye. One of the saddest things about HIV/AIDS is the effect it can have within families when things are not talked about. It makes the grieving so much more difficult for those left behind. But of course, the wishes of the person who has HIV/AIDS must be respected above all.

I spent a lot of time with one family, and we are to this day firm friends. I won a mystery flight in a competition and took their son with me. We set out at five in the morning and ended up in Sydney for the day, visiting Taronga Park Zoo, eating ice cream on the steps of the Opera House, exploring The Rocks and lying on the grass at Circular Quay talking about his family, his lover, his life before HIV/AIDS, how to heal the world—anything and everything. We laughed a lot; he asked the most ridiculous riddles, which I had no hope of solving! He died four months later. That day in Sydney is one of the happy memories of a very dear, warm young man that I take with me to the candlelight vigil every year. I wish I could say he is the only one.

Being in that support group was very rewarding, not only for the friendships that were formed. There is strength in numbers, even if the number is only two, and I saw at first-hand how sharing a mutual adversity could enable the human spirit to endure pain beyond the imagination of most. There is better, more intelligent information available these days, and people giving freely of their time and expertise in care and support groups, and I hope to be able to make useful contribution wherever I can.

Of course this is only a quick dip into the changes brought to my life when my son came out and took me with him into the gay community. I have made some good friends, and done things I would most likely never have had a chance to do if he had been heterosexual. I probably would never have marched in a candlelight vigil under a PFLAG banner or marched in a peace rally in Brisbane under a Gays For Peace banner. I probably would never have met the dedicated PFLAG-ers at Midsumma Festival in Melbourne and joined their group. My life is richer for all these things and I hope I can always welcome and enjoy what is different, and those who are different and dare to be so for all the world to see.

If my story brings a little reassurance and understanding or a new train of thought to ease someone's mind, I will be more than satisfied. I've kept it short deliberately, but I hope I have given enough to ease the very natural feelings of apprehension, uncertainty, isolation and doubt you may have. If we realise that these feelings are often shared by both parties, we are well on the way to understanding and accepting things as they are. As I said earlier, it takes time, but exchanging experiences and ideas with each other, such as in a PFLAG meeting, or one to one, can make it easier.

*Written by a mother from Newcastle, New South Wales.*

I am grateful to have this opportunity to express my feelings about my son's sexuality and hope that any parent reading this letter who is having trouble accepting will benefit from my experience.

I guess from the time David was very small I knew he was special. He had ways about him that were very endearing not only to his parents and family, but to many that he met. His gentle artistic ways were evident in those early years. He was not keen, like his older brother, to kick the football around the lawn or have a hit of cricket, but loved his weekly lessons at a local theatre where they taught drama and dance. We encouraged this, as we could see he had some talent in this field, the same as we encouraged his brother at sport and sister at ballet. This was the pattern for many years and little did I realise how much pain he was suffering through the rejection from some of his peers at school. He was a boy with a great sense of humour and person-ality and I always felt he held his own and was well liked, which I think was true up to a point, but the remarks and cruelty which young ones can show was always evident and it was not until he went to boarding school that we fully realised his problems of not being accepted. I think back now and feel not only guilt but much sadness to think I was unable to help him during those critical years, but he was unable to confide at that stage in his life to anyone.

I have to admit that when he could no longer keep his secret and told my husband and myself, I reacted badly, for which I feel much shame. It should not have come as such a shock, for I knew. I guess, at the time I did not want to hear.

Now the truth had erupted, I agonised for some time as to why he was like this. Was it because I had suffered the loss of my mother during pregnancy with him, and did I treat him differently from my older children? Should we have forced him to participate in more 'manly' activities? These thoughts were always with me and my fears for his future were very daunting. His life would be abnormal; he wouldn't enjoy the pleasure of having a family of his own; he would be shunned by his peers; he would lead a lonely life. All these fears were with me for some years and I felt unable to tell even my closest friends for some time. I guess I felt ashamed and thought everyone would be shocked. Gradually I confided in a few friends and they were so supportive it made me realise how foolish I had been. David was still the same David and I realised it was not going to make any difference to the relationship he had with his family and friends.

We have all come a long way—we have each accepted and grown from the experience. Our son has matured with confidence in who he is and where he is going. My husband and I have so much love and admiration for our son and are proud to say he is gay.

*Written by a mother in her late fifties from Brisbane.*

I have two children, both boys in their mid-thirties. I was very hopeful for grandchildren coming along eventually. When my eldest son was sixteen, he went on a school trip to Sydney for four days. When he came home, it was with a different set of friends. I started to get suspicious, and this went on for twelve months. I finally got it out of him, and you can understand how upset I was—it didn't do my blood pressure any good. I didn't know how I was going to tell my husband. When I did, he was disgusted and could not bear to talk or even think about it. Of course, it did not make things very easy between us. I said to him, if he couldn't accept it, he would have to learn to live with it. It doesn't exist as far as he's concerned. But we have had several years to cope with it now. But then we got another blow.

At 30, our other son tells us that he is too. It broke my heart, as he and I have always been close. He was in denial! He does not want to be. He recently found a friend and seems happy about it. I can only hope. They both have had some lovely girlfriends and still have. The elder has a nice house and friends. I worry so much about HIV though. It's always in the back of my mind. I can only hope they are very careful. All of this still does not stop the hurt we feel over it all. I lost my mother when I was ten years old and my father when I was 21. My husband lost his father when he was 21 months old. We really would have liked to have grandchildren, but no such luck. I can only hope they keep healthy.

*Written by a mother from Adelaide. Born in the UK to parents who were loving, gentle, conservative people. Both died of cancer by the time she was 21.*

*A childhood dream was finally realised when she arrived in Australia in 1970. She has worked all her life since leaving school at fourteen and feels that she never stops learning from people. She despises racism and supports equal rights for all.*

*Her lifelong philosophy was given to her by her parents—NEVER sit in judgement until you have put yourself firmly in the other person's shoes.*

I gave birth to a son when I was 21. Two years later I found myself listening to my husband's family making the odd joke about him. You see, the child's favourite toys, in fact the only ones he ever really played with, were his cousin's dolls and dollshouse.

It was the 'nudge, nudge, say no more' kind of joke that alerted me to the injustice of labelling our son. Well, so what? What if he did turn out like that when he grew up? Did this mean that he would have no value as a person and they would reject him? This is our son and we love him. They were happy when he was born. What the hell is going on here?

The seeds were sown in both my husband and myself to the extent where my husband drew away from the son he was so proud of, and I withdrew from my husband. I left him and turned my back on his family five years later.

We had another child when my son was three. A daughter. Wonder of wonders, he had his own real live doll. He adored her then as he does now, almost 30 years later. The three of us have shared much heartbreak over the years and many injustices, but always . . . always we have shared a tremendous love, respect and strength in each other and would join forces to work things out together. I have learned more from these children born to me than from anyone else in my life.

We have no contact with any of my family either. We have no need to justify ourselves. We have good friends, and my son has a wonderful brother-in-law and his family who are accepting. These are people specially chosen who are important to us. They quite possibly don't understand my son's sexual preference, but it is never an issue either. They know him and like him for who he is and they accept him as part of their own family.

I guess my own in-built curiosity to learn from and accept people for who they are, along with trying to keep an open mind on all things, has educated me about gays, lesbians, transsexuals, cross-dressers etc. My son was born into a handicap—not a physical or psychological one of his own, but a handicap thrust on him by an uneducated, fearful society. As with any handicap, it takes great strength of character to overcome it. I will challenge that every family has at least one member who is not 'straight down the line', but has to either hide away in the closet, believing they are unworthy of love from their family, or move to another part of the country or world to protect themselves from those they love.

I have learned enough to fill a book about the many diversities that exist within the gay and lesbian community, but the one thing that sets them apart from the heterosexual counterparts is their honesty. Oh yes, the heterosexual community has equally as many diversities, and in much greater numbers. These are the people who live in fear of being found out and who live with guilt, frustration and lies. These are your friends, neighbours, fellow parents, family, shopkeepers. They are 'straight', so you never suspect, do you?

I have moved within the gay and lesbian community for many years now. I respect their honesty and their courage. Please stop for a moment and acknowledge the sheer guts it takes them to confront their own sexuality. They have struggled alone for many years with an inner conflict and have tried desperately hard to conform to the 'norm'. Many even marry and have children before they are able to admit, even to themselves, that they can no longer live this lie. This is a living hell. Even my own son (who told me when he was fourteen) struggled for a long time before he told me. He said, 'I knew you were accepting of other people, but I didn't know if you could accept your own son.' Yes, I will defend their right to be out and proud to my dying day. I myself am out and proud as a parent.

I have little sympathy for anyone who will turn their back on their own son, daughter, sister or brother and hide behind religion or whatever in order to uphold a self-righteous image. Nature alone dictates their sexual preference, not family members. At this point in their lives they would give anything to change the way things are, but they cannot. To you I am going to ask one very important question. Did you love this person before you knew? If the answer is yes, then clearly the problem is your own. Help is at hand and if you can join forces with the one you love, to help each other, then you have cemented a bond that will give you both strength and tremendous pride in each other.

You may find that you have to reprioritise your friends and family, but that too will be a test of their love and loyalty for you, as yours is tested for the one you love. Truth and honesty can be a great cleanser and leveller and we all stand to benefit from it.

How many gays and lesbians do you know? It is fear of the unknown generally that disables people's judgement. Please contact any gay or lesbian community hotline and ask for assistance. Just get out there and meet some of these wonderful people. That is just what they are—people. They will be the ones to help you most and they will help you at your own pace. Trust them, you will learn much. It takes courage and lots of unselfish love. You will be rewarded in many ways. My love and support go with you and your loved one.

*Written some years ago by Janine Rouse of Christchurch, New Zealand. Janine and her husband, Graham, have a family of six boys—three are from her previous marriage and three are from her husband's previous marriage. All of the boys are in their twenties now and have left the nest.*

I found myself last October doing just what was usual for me—rejoicing in the anticipation of long summer days and balmy evenings after a gruelling winter. I was also spring-cleaning in many areas of my life, having changed direction in career, and I now took a week off to prepare for the transition. Life at home was every bit as demanding as at work and our six sons, four of them teenagers, had provided an area of challenge that expanded daily into many new ways of looking at life in general and our responsibilities as concerned parents in such a changing world.

An inveterate list maker, I began making a list for this week of 'stocktaking' and, among the many chores, I found I was thinking also of the many personal areas of my life I must deal with now. Letters to friends long neglected, an outing for a convalescing friend, and then there was Simon, my son of eighteen years—the oldest boy of my first marriage and so much pleasure to me. An intelligent, articulate boy, he had become my friend as we had shared a mutual interest in music and literature. Having flown through school with good academic results, he was working before embarking on a university degree, yet over his adolescent years he had grown more withdrawn and even a little secretive.

I had remarried some six years before and although Simon didn't seem to find this too difficult at the time, and welcomed the man who became a great friend to him too, he was able to hide amongst the extended family scene and become a loner. I was concerned about his loneliness and more and more concerned at his lack of social skills with his peers. He didn't have any girlfriends and had only one close friend at the all-male school he went to. Although a good friend, he was never part of Simon's weekend activities.

Gradually it began to dawn on me that all was not well with Simon and I needed to find out what troubled him. Some mothers have an innate ability to sense the worries of their offspring and I was constantly being nudged by the thought of the possibility of Simon being gay. It was too abhorrent to even contemplate, and I had pushed away this idea for many years, but each time it recurred I was able to instantly recall a moment when one of my dear brothers had been very vocal in telling Simon to 'not be a sissy' when Simon refused to play rugby with him. I remember thinking then that rugby definitely wasn't Simon's thing and told my brother that 'Simon's different.' 'Oh, hell!' he laughed. 'I'd watch that if I were you!'

But I hadn't been able to admit to myself that what I had watched over the years had been just that—a difference; and now here we were a few months away from Simon's eighteenth birthday and the 'difference' in Simon was simply that he was morose, withdrawn and terribly unhappy.

So at the end of my week's spring-cleaning, when all had been crossed off my list of things to do, I now faced what has been one of the hardest moments of my life. I simply had to know if Simon was gay. I had wrestled all week with the probability that he might be going to answer yes and I was terrified of hearing that. My courage was hauled up from the depths with just one thought—If he is, then he must be going through HELL! Like a mother tending a grazed knee, I knew that I could ease that hell.

I couldn't plan the time and venue, though I knew it was private and uninterrupted time we needed for this. That time simply appeared one calm and sunny afternoon when I had just farewelled my colleagues from my previous job after a lovely lunch together in the sun. Simon's job had unexpectedly finished early and there he was, and there I was, and there was the moment.

How grateful I was for our closeness, because it was always an instant hug and warm greeting with him, which that day both of us needed. I held onto that for a long time before sitting him down close to me and quietly telling him I had been concerned about him and wondered if his unhappiness has been because he was afraid to share something with me. His expression was instantly aloof and a little defensive. Somehow I persevered and eventually asked him, 'Are you gay?'

It seems such a happy word, but what torment it had been for Simon. He burst into tears and clung to me, shaking uncontrollably with huge sobs of relief, gratitude and even apology. 'I didn't know how to tell you,' he wept. 'I've been so confused. I'm sorry Ma, I'm sorry!'

We comforted each other. I rocked him instinctively like a baby and he patted my back reassuringly. Love pats we call them in our family. It seemed ages that we sat there together. When our tears were calmer we began to talk and openly share with a new-found honesty which I felt so reassured by. I needed to know when he first realised that he was a homosexual and if he had had a homosexual experience. I also needed him to know that I loved him just as much and he must know that, whatever was to cross his path in the years to come, I would always love him and be there for him.

Children began to drift in from school and while we continued to sit on, our mammoth emotions spent, a quiet relief filtered over both of us. I looked around and realised with some incredulity that nothing had changed. I am here, the sun is shining, the garden is a delight—it is all as it was a few moments ago.

For days I floated on a cloud of relief. Relieved that I knew now, relieved that Simon could be free—it was like the dreamy nether world I had floated around in after the news that my young, fit father had dropped dead suddenly, years before. My grief then was to come much later, when full realisation of his loss came to me. And so it was with Simon. Out of the blue beyond came the most devastating grief imaginable. Having pragmatically discussed with Simon such things as safe sex, not being promiscuous, being honest in a relationship, not using people, choosing a partner well and carefully—suddenly I felt tremendous loss. Loss of a son, loss of unspoken dreams and ambitions I had for his future, and loss of a child. He was now a mature, sexually-aware adult and his lover would be a man.

My husband provided a warmth and support at this time, as his previous marriage had broken up after the discovery of his wife's lesbianism. It seemed like a double blow to him and with my need to lean on him for support was also a desire to protect him from it all.

I began to meet some of Simon's friends. They were normal men, not camp or effeminate as I had always imagined homosexuals were. I clung to things to be grateful for.

During this time Simon shared very honestly with us all that was happening to him. We talked about the things that really mattered; our feelings, his feelings, and through it all a tremendous enrichment of our already solid relationship began to emerge. He laughed with us, cried with us and then left us to live with his lover.

A very great need developed for someone to talk to who had been through the same thing, but where to find this? Yellow Pages, newspapers, public libraries and the Citizens Advice Bureau could all give us loads of leads to follow if WE were gay, but not if we were parents of a gay child. Simon had been born in an age where homosexuality was becoming an accepted part of our society and even parliamentary statutes legislating an end to discrimination were being passed, but where were all the parents of these freed men and women? With growing sadness I realised that the new-found freedom enabling all of these gay people to come out of the closet had made parents, relatives and in some cases friends run for the very closet doors that had freed their children, to imprison themselves behind the doors of shame. 'What will the neighbours think?', 'How will I tell my family?'— questions arising from the years of subtle conditioning which confronts us all with our strong bias towards heterosexuality. There was going to be a lot to overcome!

I am gradually freeing myself from some of the crippling myths of homosexuality that I had gathered along my life's path, and through quiet patience I am enjoying a new perspective on my capacity for change, for suggestion and above all for honesty.

I believe we are never given anything in life which we are unable to withstand and by the quiet settling of our pain comes home a gratitude for the understanding that through new-found strengths come also rewards aplenty.

That's what parenthood is really isn't it? Painful, but reward-ing!

*This letter was written by Janine some time ago, and following is an update.*

This letter is really light-years away from where I am now in my thinking on the subject!!

Graham and I have really had to question deeply how we had arrived at our various opinions on the aspects of homosex-uality and the moral and ethical dynamics involved.

We discovered much conditioning, both parental and societal, which had formed the basis of our knowledge and therefore our beliefs. We had to admit to being homophobic. The eventual dispelling of the homophobia and the myths etc. came about through reading and talking with gay men and women and then a conscious 'coming out' as a parent of a gay son. What 'freedom' this allowed. No longer shackled with fears of prejudice or non-acceptance, but a realisation of the importance of not allow-ing the opinions of others to affect Simon.

The area most in conflict at that time was my long-held Protestant beliefs and attendance at church. I was unable to find any fellow parishioners or clergy willing to accept Simon as a welcome member of worship services. Indeed, they were very solicitous in offers of help to 'cure' him!! This was absolutely unacceptable to me and I ceased church worship. However, that did not answer my own need to continue in my own spiritual development and I was led to the right place quite soon.

I now attend our local Christian Science church, founded by Mary Baker-Eddy in the mid-1800s. It has a universal concept of man as being spiritual and not material, as already-perfect ideas of God, not needing to be forgiven for any sin; here in material form simply to work out our spiritual existence and inheritance. Here Simon is welcomed as a perfect child of God. There is no judgement of any kind and there is warm acceptance and a peaceful environment for spiritual growth.

All the siblings (Simon is the eldest of six boys) accept him as he is. So do our friends and neighbours! There is still prejudice about in our communities and as proud parents of proud gay children we feel we can (in a loving way) cause people to really be truthful about how they do, or do not, accept being gay as being OK!! We enjoy the debates and respect everyone's opinions, but there is always the aim to cause the world to question itself and not the gay members of society.

Through Simon's coming out, I have 'come out' of my former limited view of what it means to be gay. Simon asked me once, 'When did you decide to be heterosexual?' Good question, I thought, one that truly puts to rest the still prevalent thinking that homosexuality is a preference or chosen way of life—not so!

I feel truly blessed and enriched greatly having had this experience to grow through with Simon. It has better enabled me to truly know myself. I have especially learned to accept others and to only see the goodness and truth that is in all people. The resulting love is unconditional and ever present.

*Written by a mother from a country town in Western Australia. She enjoyed every moment of bringing up her three children, even though her husband was often absent due to work commitments. They enjoy a close relationship with their married son and daughter and have a special place in their hearts for their younger son.*

When we received a letter from our son earlier this year addressed to my husband and I, my first thought was, This is a letter to tell us he is gay. I was not surprised and neither was my husband, but we had not shared these thoughts before. I know both of us, in our own way, thought that if we didn't talk about it, these suspicions would go away. I also didn't feel that I should pry, and that if our son was gay, he would tell us when he was ready. I don't know that this was a good idea and my main guilt feeling now is that I didn't try to find out earlier, so that we could have tried to support our son over the years. He has had so long not knowing how and when to tell us. He must have felt very alone. I am very sorry about that. Even now, though, it seems a little unreal.

Why are people gay? I don't know, but I am sure they wouldn't choose to be gay if they could help it. I feel sad sometimes that our son is not going to marry and have children, our grandchildren, like his brother and sister have. We love him dearly; he is a wonderful son and he rings us regularly and has always stayed in touch in a very caring way. I know he loves us very much.

Because he lives in Melbourne, we still have a lot of adjusting to do to accept his lifestyle. We have not been closely involved with his friends. I worry about the hurts that he must already have suffered, when he couldn't share them with us. I'm concerned about the future in a society that is yet to totally accept him and concerned that so many gay people contract AIDS. Health is just so precious.

I am having trouble deciding how and when to share with our friends and extended family that our son is gay. I don't know how I should feel about this. He is such a friendly, likeable person. Our friends always ask after him. I guess I don't want them to change their attitude towards him and think any less of him as a person, just because he is gay.

The youngest of our three children, our son has great support from his older brother and his wife, who has a sister who is gay. He felt able to tell them quite some time before he told us. I'm very grateful that they were there for him. He also has unconditional love from his sister and brother-in-law. He has three nephews and three nieces who adore him.

I know this is just the beginning, and because we have such love and admiration for this wonderful young man, we hope we can show enough love and understanding and learn to deal with the problems that we may have to face. We have a very special young man in our family.

To all parents I can only say: life is precious, whatever colour, creed or sexual preference is our lot. Don't throw it away.

*Written by a mum from rural Victoria who has been married for twenty years. She has raised three boys, the eldest of whom is gay.*

Recently I had what felt at the time like one of the most painful experiences a parent could endure. My teenage son had become more and more withdrawn and seemed somehow terribly sad. I had a very strong gut feeling that something was terribly wrong. I made him sit and talk with me. I was determined to find out what was bothering him, and finally he began to open up. 'Well, Mum, I think I may have finally found someone who could be special, but you won't be happy about it!'

Waves of fear began to crash through me. I remember praying, 'Maybe it will be an older woman with ten kids to support,' because instinctively I knew what I was about to hear. 'Why wouldn't I be happy?' I whispered. 'Because I think you spoke to him on the phone the other night.'

My heart felt as though it was ripped right out of my body—the pain was as intense as anything I've ever known. (I can best describe it as being similar to what I felt when my mother died.) What followed was the most dramatic, traumatic and draining couple of hours, and then days and weeks of forcing myself out of bed each day, functioning as best I could, pretending everything was as usual—working, mothering my other children, cooking, cleaning, interacting with other people, being a wife— my heart shattered, my world destroyed! (I thought.)

Like many others I know now, I was homophobic, frightened and ignorant of what 'their' world was like, feeling sure it was decadent, immoral, sick and totally depraved.

I went to a psychologist, and, weeping, expecting my feelings to be verified (I guess), told her how I would never be able to accept him bringing home a partner, that I hated the idea of 'poofs' even walking hand in hand in public.

She patiently explained that this was not a 'choice', that if they could choose, no one would ever subject themselves to such pain, such torment. She explained that through her work she had come to believe that homosexuality was something predestined at conception, a genetic defect, inexplicable, and no blame could ever be placed on this unfortunate dear son of mine, and none should be placed on anyone. She made me see that the problem of acceptance was mine, that my son would more than ever need my love and support, that surely this was only a small part of him, that he was still the same son I had always known—words that were an echo of those he had spoken when trying to console me.

I came away knowing she was right, but how do I tell his father? He is a true homophobic, who uses lines like, 'Poofs should be all put away.' I have no doubt about my love for my son, not for what he is but for who he is. He is a gentle person, but also hard working, ambitious, dedicated, kind, supportive, generous and a positive, happy-natured boy who I'm proud to have brought into the world, even though now I ache to think of the painful road ahead of him. A lifetime of dealing with bigoted, small-minded people in their LITTLE worlds, and the main one may be his own father! Can I bear remaining in the middle of them forever as mediator, a position I've often found myself in over the years? I don't feel strong enough! I decided I needed to ease my mind about the dangerous environment he was entering.

By pure chance a close friend and I found ourselves being attended to by a very well-spoken Russian waiter at a restaurant in Melbourne. I had whispered to Deirdre, 'I think he is gay.'

'You're paranoid!' she answered.

After we'd eaten I said to him, 'Is there anywhere close by that we could enjoy some entertainment?' He pondered for a while and then said, 'If you want a hassle-free night, there is a "poofs" club nearby.' Seeing the irony in that, we cracked up. Looking bemused, he went on. 'You will be very safe there and they have great music!' I asked him to come with us, saying I felt like I could trust him.

'Yes,' he said, 'I am gay, you are safe with me!' To cut a long story short, we talked for hours. I explained my son's recent revelation and he helped me understand many things. I asked him if it was too much to ask my son to try heterosexual sex. He answered that for some it could be a very traumatic experience. He said, 'For example, how would you feel about someone suggesting you have sex with a woman?' It had not occurred to me to look at it like that. He also told me about a group within the gay community called 'Survival' who educate young gays about AIDS and who teach them how to cope in 'LIFE' situations, that is deal with aggression towards them etc.

He told me about his early years and how desperately he wanted to fit in, to be 'mainstream', to be so-called 'normal'. I might add the music was good and the place was safe. Our bags were checked before we were allowed in (for drugs, he explained). The place was packed with very well-dressed, well-behaved young men and women. I remember thinking they are all somebody's sons and daughters, somebody's sisters and brothers, and I wondered then how many had parents that knew the truth?

I am so glad and proud that my son had enough faith in my continued love and support to tell me.

I read recently that one-third of all young suicides are committed by gay people. I have a simple message, something someone said to me—it is 'LOVE YOUR CHILDREN', and from me I add, don't be judgemental, be compassionate of others. You just never know when it could happen to your family.

In a way I feel like a better person somehow for having experienced this, not that I would 'CHOOSE' for us to be going through it, but it has opened my mind and my heart, and I know I have grown emotionally because of it, and even though the future is daunting, I wouldn't want to live a 'LITTLE' life.

When I told my closest girlfriend she said, 'God, is that all? I thought he must be dying or something. You've still got to love him—he's still the same boy!' My sister-in-law said, 'If my son grows up to be half the person he is, I'll be so proud.'

I believe there is a minority group of radicals within the gay community who are out there being blatant and offensive (i.e. the behaviour of some in the Gay Mardi Gras in Sydney could be an example) about their sexuality; and 'straight' people do get a bad impression, believing all gays behave like this. My small experience is that this is a minority, and most do not behave that way in public. I still think sex is private, be it heterosexual or homosexual, and should be treated as such. Whatever is publicly acceptable for heterosexuals should be OK for gays, including affectionate behaviour within the boundaries of decency. Why is it so hard for us to accept? I'm learning to.

A loving mother.

*This letter was written by Coral-Lea Benzie, who has been happily married to Jim for 30 years. They have three children—a daughter, Kate, who is married (with a little girl and boy), and two sons, Tim and Garnet.*

*Coral-Lea says, 'Always remember they are still the same children you have always had.'*

I thought long and hard about how to write this letter until one day while reading a story to our grandchildren I realised, what better way to tell a fairy story than with 'once upon a time'.

Once upon a time there lived a happy married couple called Coral-Lea and Jim. They had three lovely children, called Kate, Tim and Garnet, who coped with the usual traumas of childhood and the dramas of being teenagers. Actually, they were really great kids, well behaved and achieving well at school and university. I suppose as parents Coral-Lea and Jim were probably quite smug about what a good job they had done. Until . . .

As you may have guessed, my name is Coral-Lea and our son Tim is gay. I will try and relate how Tim told us he was gay and all the emotions and consequences we experienced.

I remember well when Tim came out to us. For a start, I didn't even know what 'coming out' meant. It was June and he was home on holidays from an acting course he was doing in Melbourne. He'd finished his bachelor of arts the year before at the University of Queensland, and although we'd noticed a change in him we had no idea what he was going through. His 21st birthday was coming up in October and we'd all had a lovely week together, but there were times when I noticed he was a little uptight. We found out later why . . .

As he left the house one night he said he needed to speak to Jim and I about something really important to him when he returned. As he was so serious, we spent quite a few apprehensive hours wondering what the problem was. Tim had never been one to cause any problems, in fact quite the opposite. He was a wonderful student, very popular and a great achiever in anything he tackled. Most importantly, he was kind and considerate to all he came in contact with—a wonderful and loving son who we were both very close to and indeed proud of.

Finally he arrived home with the saddest face I have ever seen. He didn't come straight out and tell us he was gay but said he was a fraud and not everything we thought him to be. He kept asking us if we could guess what the problem was. Of course we went through the usual things like alcohol and drugs and then finally I asked if it was to do with girls. I had hit the nail on the head. Tim told us he was gay. He sobbed, I cried and Jim looked devastated. It was a shattering experience, to say the least. We will always be grateful that Tim told us together. It must be terribly hard for one parent to have to tell another or carry the secret of knowing on their own for a while. Tim asked had we ever suspected that he was gay and I remember once thinking that it was strange that Tim had had so many girlfriends but the relationships never amounted to anything. The thought went through my mind but I pushed it aside, thinking I was being ridiculous.

One of the saddest things about that night was the fact that Tim had arranged to go to a friend's house in case we threw him out. I couldn't believe that he would think we wouldn't accept him. We had loved and supported him all his life in everything he had done. It is such a tragedy that some families do in fact throw their children out. After a sleepless night we went to see our local doctor, who suggested we visit a psychologist. Tim was quite angry and upset about this because he thought we were trying to change his mind. He came with us because I thought we needed someone to help us sort out our feelings. There seemed to be no one else to talk to. You feel so alone at this time because usually none of your family or friends appear to have gay children and it is not something you bring up casually over a cup of coffee, although I do this now quite easily.

I remember once a friend asking me if Tim had a girlfriend, because he is quite tall and so is her daughter. I said no, actually he has a boyfriend. We have a good laugh over that now but I realise now it was a bit mean to spring the news on her that way. As you can see, I don't have any problems now with the fact that Tim is gay. It seems quite silly now but I even found it hard to say the word 'gay' at first. I really feel that it is important to talk about your child—the more people that know, the easier it will be for some other child to tell their parents.

Tim went back to Melbourne to continue his studies and we continued on with our lives. I think parents go through a grieving period, probably because you feel that everything has changed and life is not going to continue the way you expected it to. I went through all different emotions. 'Anger'—why are you doing this to us? 'Guilt'—because I didn't know the anguish he was going through while he was coming to terms with his sexuality. 'Regret'—what could we have done differently, should we have insisted he play more sports? This sounds funny now but everyone seems to say it and I always chuckle when I hear it. Thank goodness for the rugby league footballer, Ian Roberts, who came out quite recently. 'Fear'—how can I possibly tell my family and friends? You don't want them to think any less of your child or think you've been a bad parent. I realised through all of this the most important emotion of all is love.

Once I realised that I loved Tim unconditionally and nothing else mattered I was once again on firm ground. Tim was still the same person, nothing had changed except he was attracted to men, not women. Once you start telling friends and family, you feel as if you have lost a great weight off your shoulders. It gets easier if you remember how much you love your child, and if other people don't like it, that's their problem. I always think that at some time in their life they too may have a child, a grandchild, a niece or nephew that is gay.

We've certainly come a long way in the many years since Tim came out to us. I remember feeling quite apprehensive when I met a boyfriend of Tim's for the first time. I wondered how I would deal with it. He was just as nervous as I was and we became firm friends.

To finish our fairy story, our Prince Charming has met his Cinderfella and is living happily ever after.

*This letter was written by my mother, who has recently moved from Sydney to the South Coast of New South Wales. She now lives in a*

*lazy, picturesque seaside town about two hours south of Sydney, which induces a sense of relaxation. Mum is settling in well and making lots of friends at the local Anglican church and through various social groups. Mum turned 67 in early 1998 and it is great to see her continuing to embrace life and living each day to the full.*

*She is a beautiful woman who I saw go through a lot when her marriage fell apart in the late seventies and early eighties. Although in much pain, she dragged herself through the break-up without breaking down. Her strong motherly instinct somehow gave her power to continue to bring up my two older brothers and me. Dad had left her for a woman twenty years younger. Mum was left to run their business and somehow she still found time to give Scott, Wayne and me plenty of love. The three of us at the time were typical teenage boys, pretty much oblivious to her stress levels. Nearly twenty years on, I look back and wonder how Mum coped. I can now see that the parent I thought was weak was in fact steadfast strong, and this is something I love very much about her. Surely anyone else would have crumbled.*

*Mum had a very protected childhood, being brought up in a strict fundamentalist Baptist family. She had always lived by the Biblical edict that the man is the head of the house, and when any problem seemed unsolvable, Dad would have the final say. Dad was strong and very inflexible. I sometimes wonder if Mum's true personality, desires and aspirations may have been thwarted through her very protected childhood and subsequently in her marriage, where at times I believe Dad tended to be oppressive.*

*She became a much stronger person through the break-up. Today she is wiser, more understanding of differences and more in touch with the reality of life. Her eyes have been opened to much and although she has been hurt, I believe she is better for it. She does what she wants now, which is good for her.*

*She seems to have taken a very strict fundamentalist church-based stance in her following letter. Sadly, I don't think it gets across the extent of the warmth we have in our relationship.*

*I love Mum very much and I know she dearly loves me. We disagree on some things and although that can make it hard, I should know better than anyone to accept each other's different beliefs and opinions . . . and I try to. She may be right and I wrong, or I may be right and she wrong, but chances are, I think, that we are probably both right on some things and off the mark on others. Isn't that always the case?*

*Despite how frustrating I find parts of Mum's letter, I hope by including it, other fundamentalist Christian readers will find useful insights.*

I am writing this letter because as your mother I must say the things that are in my heart. I do not intend to write things that will necessarily please you, but I want you to know that I write as I do simply because I love you so much.

You are the youngest of my three boys, who are all very precious to me, and I love you all dearly.

As I look back over the past years, I think of you all with your own special gifts and personalities and I thank you all for the joy you have brought me—sometimes mixed with pain, but that is part of life and what growing up is all about.

Life was pretty good as I watched you all growing up in our country home, and I suppose, like most mothers, I used to dream of what you might all become one day. We seemed to have everything, didn't we, as you were growing up—a lovely home, big cars, a business, overseas trips and all the things that money can buy. To an onlooker we must have appeared to be the perfect family, but while everything always looked good on the outside, the devil had been working for many years, breaking down family values and commitments until finally you boys became the victims of another failed marriage.

Failure in marriage was something that was totally foreign to me. I believed that vows made before God were sacred and that when two people were joined in marriage it was to be a lifelong union. I had seen that in my parents' and grandparents' marriages and it was beautiful.

When my marriage collapsed, I was completely devastated and found it a bitter pill to swallow. I wallowed in self-pity for many years. It did not hit me at the time how much you boys must have been suffering and for this I ask your forgiveness. I know now the pain you must have gone through and I believe, Bryce, that at age twelve you were greatly affected by having witnessed at such a critical age what must have been a terribly confused picture of what love was all about. All the things you had been taught could not have made sense to you at the time—it must have seemed like total hypocrisy.

Just when you needed a solid family relationship as part of the normal development process of growing up, there was none. You needed so much the fulfilment a normal, loving family gives, but these needs were not met at a time when you needed them most. I really have agonised over this so much, and again I ask your forgiveness for anything that I might have said or done which in any way might have affected your thinking.

You were always a very sensitive and loving person so I can imagine what you must have gone through before you finally asked your father and I, a few years later, to meet you so that we could have a talk. That was when you told us that you believed you were homosexual. My reaction at the time was total disbelief that a son of mine could ever think this way, let alone talk about acting on it. I found it hard to come to terms with what you were saying.

I don't believe you got any help from either of your parents at this time, as we just could not handle it. In retrospect I wish that I could have talked to somebody about it—especially to a Christian mother who might have been through a similar experience, but I did not know anybody. Please forgive us for the way we must have come across to you at that time, but please remember that there was no lack of love. In fact, I loved you all the more because you were hurting and I just longed to be able to help you.

I guess we were all hurting terribly, particularly you, Bryce, because you were telling us that you had made this decision to follow a lifestyle that you felt was your 'lot in life', but I believe that in your heart you know it was not right. It made me feel so sad for you, to hear you talk like this. When a mother sees her child suffering in any way she just wants to make it better, but this was a hard one to deal with.

It has been said that homosexuality involves both a state of incompletion and a drive towards completion and I believe this to be very true.

The parent-child relationship is God's natural plan for human development, and when this is not met in some way there remains such an unfulfilled need that I can understand a person looking for love and acceptance with someone of the same sex. I believe, too, that many homosexuals are probably seeking affection and acceptance more than sex. The developmental needs involved in the homosexual condition seem natural and normal when one looks for acceptance, but the expression of these needs are certainly not!

I think this is when the devil is really having a great time these days, convincing young people that there is an alternative lifestyle. God never made us that way—He made male and female only, so that in marriage they may be joined as one. We are physically and mentally made that way—one completes the other.

I believe that our society today has become so accustomed to evil that our eyes are blinded to the reality of sin. It is made to look so attractive, to the point where one accepts sin as being normal and righteousness looks drab and strange.

The way we think determines the way we are and it would seem that homosexual behaviour becomes a habit and a lifestyle after it has been learned and practised. Doesn't the Bible say that whoever commits sin is a slave of sin (John 8: 34)? So in other words, sin is addictive. We can all relate to that as we have been slaves of sin since childhood, in some form or another. We do something once, it feels good, so we do it again and it becomes easier until finally we are hooked. It becomes an addiction just like the alcohol or drug user.

I am aware, Bryce, of how you struggled in the early days and did seek help, but I believe you were trying to do it in your own strength. Right at the heart of every person's sin problem, no matter what it is, there is a self-habit that can only be broken by Christ's help. He alone has the power to transform us.

I do not believe that sin is measured or graded—we are all sinners, especially me. We were born in sin and everyone has the potential to commit any crime. Bryce, I do not judge you in any way—only God is our judge—but I do know that you and your mother are both sinners, one no different from the other, and one's sin no greater than the other in God's sight. His heart is aching for you, longing to see you come back to the One you professed to be your Lord and Saviour.

I have found that He has never let me down, even though I have failed Him time and time again. During all the hard times when I couldn't see the way ahead for the tears, He carried me. Do you remember that beautiful verse 'Footprints' which you once gave me? I really cherished that verse because it expressed so beautifully what I had experienced, and you were sensitive enough to realise this.

Remember that God never condemns homosexuals as people, but He does say their sexual behaviour is wrong. When Jesus was on Earth, He seemed to show special compassion towards those caught up in sexual sin. God loves you, the person He made with all the special gifts and potential you have, and I just long to see you achieve sexual wholeness in Christ. That might mean celibacy, perhaps you will still be emotionally homosexual, or perhaps one day you will become a heterosexual marriage partner, but whatever happens, I only want God's best for your life, no matter what it takes.

I commit you into God's care and I am trusting Him for your salvation. I cannot stop you from pursuing the lifestyle you have chosen, but I trust a faithful God who has promised to hear and answer prayer. Therefore I will continue to pray for you as I always have done, every day of my life.

My hope comes from 1 Corinthians 6: 9–11, where Paul is speaking to people who had previously been living in the same lifestyle, and he says, 'That is what some of you were. But you were washed, you were sanctified, you were justified in the name of the Lord Jesus Christ and by the Spirit of our God.'

May it be so for you, my beloved son.

With all my love . . . Mum.

# MY STORY

At five years of age I would have been considered a normal happy kid . . . and I was. I laughed and giggled a lot, enjoyed playing games with my whole family and loved my toys. I had boundless energy and was forever running around the house singing and being silly. My brothers and I got on well and if we weren't in the yard helping Dad, we'd be competing to achieve the most dangerous feat on our bikes. I could be mischievous, like most boys, but was also very loving and affectionate. As a typical blond, freckled five-year-old, I guess I knew how to get what I wanted. What fun life was—it was like a big game and I was out to enjoy every minute of it.

They are wonderful memories. My parents were so proud of my brothers and me and we loved them trustingly in return. We had everything we wanted, and like Mum said in her letter, I guess we looked like the perfect family. It certainly felt that way to me, but I was to break their hearts in years to come.

There were things from a very early age which I could not talk about. For as far back as my memory permits, I recall being attracted to my own sex. At this age I thought my feelings were normal. I thought all boys must feel the same way. I thought girls were cute, but felt a stronger attraction towards other boys.

These feelings came naturally. In my childhood there was no dirty association—it did not feel wrong in my heart, and it was all quite innocent. The fact that nobody talked about such feelings started me wondering if I was different. As I got older I began to hear and learn what people thought of two men together. I felt forced to keep these thoughts secret as confusion developed.

I finished primary school and entered high school and puberty, and I recall hoping these feelings would go away, but they didn't. They intensified. The attraction felt good, but the torment of not being able to talk about it to anyone made it hard. I did not want to be different. I wanted to be like my mates. I wanted to be attracted to girls, but that simply did not happen. It's hard to explain what the attraction felt like. I guess it just seemed natural, probably like the attraction others feel for the opposite sex.

A sickly image of homosexuals was slowly being created in my mind. I was learning to hate part of myself. I would not have appeared lonely, but a big part of me was. My family were very religious. I went to a Christian school and was brought up in the Baptist church. These things made it harder to come to terms with my same-sex attraction.

How easy it would have been to lie to myself. I could have hidden what was in my heart, taken girls out, fallen in love with the 'perfect' woman, married her, had a family and then tried to remain faithful for the rest of my life. Always knowing what was in my heart, but living the lie. How many people feel forced to do this and pay for it later in life? I knew I couldn't do it.

The importance of being totally honest in everything was something Mum and Dad had instilled deep within me. This desire enabled me to confront my feelings. Even so, telling them was probably one of the hardest things I've ever had to do. I had been lonely with this affliction—that was what I called it at the time. I was embarrassed, hurt and confused. I felt guilty, dirty and disgusting, but an overwhelming desire to show some sort of integrity allowed me to come to Mum and Dad seeking solutions.

They considered they were showing me love when they acted out a response I sort of knew was coming. They told me I was a sinner, as we all were. They said I needed psychological help, but that did not mean I was mad. They reassured me that they were there for me as long as I tried to 'go straight'. They said I needed to meet a nice girl and that it was just a phase. They said I could overcome the influence of the devil with Jesus on my side. They wondered if it was in my mind and if I was succumbing to peer pressure. They questioned whether I was just trying to be cool. They said that through the power of God I could overcome anything.

Fortunately, fourteen years on, I understand that it is not something that has to be overcome. They said all of these things in love. That is, the love that they know. The love that they were taught in their church. It has been passed down from generation to generation. Unconditional love? . . . I don't think so. I do not agree with them, but I can empathise and understand where they are coming from. They are entitled to their personal beliefs, as much as I might not like them.

The conditioning of my upbringing and the indoctrination of the church put me through hell for many years to come. As far as sexuality goes, Mum, Dad and I disagree on a lot. That is OK though, because it is only one small part of my whole life. There are many thousands of other things on which we do agree. It's really not that hard to find common ground. The respect we have for each other might falter when it comes to certain issues, but on the whole it is overwhelmingly positive. The love I have for Mum and Dad is enormous and nothing will take that away.

I told them I was gay when I was seventeen and it took me another six years before I truly accepted it and really learned to love myself again. They don't accept my homosexuality; I guess they just put up with it. Over the years they have relearned that I am really no different from the person I was the day before I confided in them. I am still Bryce McDougall, their youngest of three boys who loves them very much.

They know a little bit more about homosexuality now and are possibly a little more tolerant, but really none of their religious beliefs have changed. I think Mum's letter says it all. She might say that I have been wrongly influenced by others, just as I believe she sometimes is. We have different views on some things, I can accept that.

I know I did the right thing in telling them. It hurt everyone deeply at the time, and although the pain has not gone away, it has lessened to a dull pain. I keep it somewhere in the back of my mind and it only pops its head up once in a while. It doesn't threaten the love I feel for my parents or that which they feel for me. It's like we just ignore that part of life. I think we have agreed to disagree. Time heals wounds.

Had I decided to hide my homosexuality from them, it would have meant keeping a whole part of my life to myself. Our relationship would not have the warmth and love it has now. It would be superficial and they would know very little about the real me. I would be hiding so many things from them. Pamela Du-Valle's 21-year-old said, 'I would rather be hated for who I am than loved for who I am not.' I guess I felt like that too.

I came out soon after I finished high school and commenced work at the Regent of Sydney hotel. I discovered very quickly that the feelings I had towards guys were not uncommon. I faced reality in a matter of months. There were many gay men working there. I could not believe they were open and honest about their sexuality. They were not embarrassed; they didn't care what others thought of them; they were funny, well liked and often good looking.

They had self-respect and in turn were respected by others. They were often exceedingly good at what they did, often paying more attention to detail then their straight colleagues, often keener to make guests feel wanted, warm and important. They were perfectly normal people. They were not 'dirty'. I had come to believe that part of me was, and I was relieved just to meet them. The biggest, most cumbersome weight of my life was lifted from my shoulders as I mixed with them and got to know them. They were loving, caring and honest.

I think many gay and lesbian people have copped such a hard time whilst growing up that they are forced to try even harder to be good at what they do. Maybe a feeling of determination triggers them to say, 'Well, I'll prove that I'm just as capable.' Terry Stewart relayed in her letter that GAY could stand for Good As You.

This determination might encourage some to become more creative, more committed, more dedicated and simply more inclined to strive for excellence. Unfortunately, there are gays and lesbians that are broken individuals who reflect none of these attributes. They are a minority, though; most strive to fit in, be successful and contribute positively to life and society.

I confided in a few of my new friends that I thought I was gay. Most people in the hotel industry had no problem with homosexuality. Many wonderful people took me under their arm as I tried to overcome the mess I was in. They were generous with their time and understanding, and very quickly became like a new family to me. They offered unconditional love and support, the likes of which I had not felt before. It was new to me then, and today I still see it as a unique quality within the gay community. I am proud of the love and support that my friends and I offer each other. My whole being changed as I came out and started to be honest with people about what I had been feeling for my whole life.

Coming out was a huge turning point in my life. It was hard but positive, scary but empowering, confronting but comforting. It was totally necessary.

You might be surprised to hear me say that I don't really think I was born gay. Neither do I believe I had a choice. I believe my sexuality developed with me as I grew. My attraction to other boys existed long before I could make informed, educated decisions. It's like it was instinctual. The feelings I had in my heart were certainly not a choice—they came naturally. (I must say that most gays and lesbians feel they were born homosexual and scientific research appears to be supporting this theory.)

My personal belief is that most people experience a varying degree of attraction to both sexes. Most would consider themselves 100 per cent attracted to the opposite sex, but I wonder if sexuality is really such a rock-solid construct. Even a 99.9 per cent attraction to the opposite sex might leave room for a confronting situation to present itself.

I'm positive I am not 100 per cent gay, but because I feel far more attraction for men than I do women, I feel I have no choice but to consider myself gay. Ideally, I wish there was no need for labels at all.

I could fall in love on an intellectual level with a woman, but sexually I would not be attracted to her. Love on this level is beautiful and although it might permit a lifelong friendship, I do not believe it is the love that relationships should be founded on. In my heart I could not totally oppress my same-sex attraction. Eventually it would manifest itself in reality. I could never do that to a woman. In a way it looks like a choice, but really there is no choice. Defeatist, you might say; I prefer to think that I am just getting on with my life.

For 31 years I've known in my heart where my true preference lies. For others, though, it can be very different and possibly harder. Consider those who are equally attracted to both sexes.

In generations to come, when homophobia is something we read about in history books, I hope we will live in a society where any two people can fall in love—whether they are of the same or opposite sex will not be of consequence.

Being gay is not the hardest thing on Earth to deal with, although it felt like it was for a long time. It is certainly easier than living in denial. I love life. There is just one major thing I would dearly love that being gay virtually prevents. I would love to have children. I feel sorry for the many thousands of sterile men and women who might feel the same. Who knows . . . maybe homosexuality is a divine safety valve to slow the world's spiralling population. (Incidentally, our world population is currently increasing by about 250 000 people every day—this statistic taken from the Population Institute.)

Being gay does not affect my ability to enjoy life to the full. Every now and then I might face a setback which could be attributed to my sexuality, but everybody faces setbacks in one way or another. Once I regain strength, I just strive on that little bit harder.

I have so much to be thankful for. I was not born mentally or physically disadvantaged. I was born in one of the most beautiful countries in the world. I have a wonderful circle of friends who are supportive in most everything I do. We share plenty of good times together. We go away for weekends, play games, have a few drinks, swim, walk, talk and, most importantly, laugh. I have a job which gives me great satisfaction. I have excellent health.

My family are close. When we get together, we inevitably have a good laugh, the nephews and niece tell a few jokes, play the piano, dance and maybe throw a ball around the backyard. We reminisce about the good old times and look forward to the future. It might be silly to say life couldn't be better, but it does feel that way. The thing I know for certain is that life could be a hell of a lot worse. I am eternally grateful for everything I have. I hope I can help others achieve greater happiness too.

Just over two and a half years ago I fell in love with my partner. Our relationship is the icing on the cake. Life felt great before we met, but it is even better now. John and I share and enjoy a wonderful life together. Sure, we have our arguments, but I think they're healthy because we are talking about what is on our minds and working through the issues. We both love and respect one another very much.

There is one thing I hope the letters have made very clear: **it is not your fault if your child is gay.** Gay kids, like straight kids, come from all classes, races and creeds. There is no one thing that causes a child to grow up gay. Some people develop outgoing personalities and others are shy; some develop confidence in some areas of their lives yet lack it in others; some develop the ability to make people laugh, others to make people contemplate life. The list is endless—we're all different. I believe it is impossible to determine why we are gay, straight or somewhere in between. Our sexuality develops with us and is probably decided long before we can consciously make a choice.

Probably one of the biggest issues gays and lesbians face is how to cope with homophobia, and for parents, too, this is clearly difficult. It is important to take the time to explore the myths that inform homophobia in society.

Below is a list of the sorts of misconceptions that arise in some people's minds when the words gay or lesbian are mentioned. They might believe that gay and lesbian people:

are suicidally unhappy
are sexually perverse
have sex in toilets
recruit homosexuals
are incapable of being successful
are effeminate if male, butch if female
talk differently
dress differently
behave differently
are not normal
are somehow responsible for the HIV virus.

The list could go on and on. It is true that some gays and lesbians are some of these things, but so are heterosexuals. It is certainly not true that all homosexuals are all of these things. You may be thinking, Well, that is an obvious statement. Unbelievably, there are people out there who think this way. Just ask any gay basher.

Between 1990 and 1995 there were 22 murders in New South Wales that were or appeared to be gay-hate-related murders. Information gathered on these murders indicates that young people under the age of 25 were involved as perpetrators in 68 per cent of cases. These statistics are taken from 'Out Of The Blue', a police survey of violence and harassment against gay men and lesbians, published in February 1995.

Many young people grow up learning to hate gays. Jason, a heterosexual friend of mine who has children of his own, was a police officer when one of these gay-hate murders was committed. He got to know one of the six convicted teenagers. Jason is an understanding, tolerant person who took the time to try and give the youth some guidance, inviting him along to meet some friends who were gay. Later, the youth asked why Jason had taken him there and Jason said that he thought it would do him good to see that they are no different from anyone else. The youth responded with, 'They weren't bad blokes.'

Where did such a strong hatred of gays come from, a hatred that led him to murder? Partly it came from his parents, but also from within his peer group, in which the need to prove masculinity is phenomenally strong. Gays are an easy target, and to leave yourself open to question by not agreeing with the peer group's mentality would take more bravery than many youths possess.

I remember reading somewhere that some gay-hate crimes have been perpetrated by persons who are unsure of their own sexuality and are in denial of their own attraction to same-sex people. What better way to try to reaffirm your own masculinity than to ridicule gays? I recall acting in a similar manner myself in high school many years ago—making fun of gays to try to put friends off the scent that I might be gay.

I believe that the roots of homophobia come from the

stereotypes some people project upon gays and lesbians. I would like to explore some of these stereotypes.

It is true that there are gays and lesbians who are suicidally unhappy. My stepbrother committed suicide several years ago and I think his inability to cope with his sexuality probably had a lot to do with it. He had been having sex with other guys, but this was probably just one of many confusing issues affecting him.

The Australian Bureau of Statistics shows that youth suicide is the second biggest killer of Australians between the ages of fifteen and 24, after motor vehicle accidents. Many road accidents might be acts of suicide too. In excess of 80 per cent of suicides in this age group are male.

Research in the United States has shown that lesbian and gay youth are two to six times more likely to attempt suicide than other youth, and they may account for 30 per cent of all completed suicides among teens.

I think that young gays and lesbians expect the worst reactions from friends and family to the news they are homosexual. From what I recall, the negative expectations were overwhelming. I could not see a way out of my problems; they seemed completely unsolvable. I guess many never even bother trying to talk as they think they know what the reactions of family, friends and society will be.

Following is an excerpt from Ann Thompson Cook's Issue paper, written for the Respect all Youth project.

A pattern of hopelessness and despair is often seen among teens who take their own lives. Many see suicide as a way to end excruciating emotional pain for which they can imagine no other solution. The cause of the pain varies from youth to youth but often includes intense family conflict, loss of someone the young person loved, or concerns or confusion about sexual identity.

A young person's sexual identity does not *itself* cause him or her to attempt suicide. Rather, the experience of growing up 'different' in a society that expects, even demands, that everyone be exclusively heterosexual can be devastating for young people who are not.

When youth realize they are lesbian, gay, or bisexual, they already know that society condemns them. Even before they reach the kindergarten playground, they learn nasty words for homosexuals. The few lesbian or gay people they have seen in movies and on television often die by suicide, homicide, or AIDS, creating disastrous expectations. Moreover, young people generally assume that all people they know are heterosexual; they have no idea that some of the healthy, respected adults around them are lesbian or gay.

Many lesbian and gay youth feel profoundly isolated: 'Surely I am the only person like this.' Some are viciously harassed and abused by peers, family members, school or agency personnel, and others. Whether or not they are labeled by others, these youth often fear being discovered and expect rejection; carefully guard their true feelings to maintain acceptance (or merely to survive); have no opportunity *openly* to date each other or flirt or engage in sexual experimenting like other teens; and lack accurate information about the normality of their feelings and experiences.

In short, they often invest tremendous energy in coping with society's negativity and discrimination. Lacking healthy adult models, skills, and support systems, many conclude they have no hope of ever becoming happy and productive. Some gay youth are in greater danger of suicide than others . . .

Kids often don't realise the impact of what they're saying. We all know that schoolchildren can be cruel to one another. What comes out of their mouths is usually just stuff they hear at home or see on TV.

For a schoolkid, coming to the realisation that they are different is difficult. Many learn to cope, but many don't. Pressure to be 'normal' is strong.

The letter from Leon's mum, on page 41, tells the story of two wonderful parents whose son attempted suicide at age seventeen. Leon's suicide note revealed that he could not live as a 'faggot' in a homophobic world. In her letter, Leon's mum says with remorse, 'I would voice my opinion in front of my children. Little did I know that my son, who had known he was gay from the age of seven or eight years, was hearing every word I said against gays and that it was cutting right into his heart. As he told me later, he didn't want to live if even his own mother thought he was bad and evil. It will take me a long time to forget the wounds I have inflicted upon my own child and it may take him a long time to regain his self-esteem.' Leon survived and the story has a positive ending, but there are many stories that don't.

We tend not to use strong words like dirty fag, sicko, poof, pillow biter or dyke around kids. It is often more subtle. We might say things like: 'Be careful of gay men, and be careful of her—she's a bit strange. Watch out for dirty men in toilets.' We might use words like queen, big girl, sissy, pansy, limp wrist or weirdo. Kids pick up every little comment and innuendo. Just the cringing and sighs of disgust a parent might show when a gay or lesbian person appears on TV are likely to be damaging. Kids learn to hate gays and lesbians, regardless of their own sexual orientation. Teenagers who find themselves attracted to the same sex might hate gays too, even though they may be gay or lesbian themselves.

It is easy to mouth off and hurt someone because we've not paused to think before we opened our mouths. An analogous example might be telling a joke about a disadvantaged person without considering that the person we're telling may have a disadvantaged brother or sister. Even worse, they might be mildly mentally disadvantaged themselves. I often put my foot in my mouth by saying unrealisingly hurtful things. It's easy to do, and it's often because I'm trying to be funny.

I don't believe that many of the things said about gays and lesbians are believed by the person who is saying them. Kids, though, listen to everything that is said, take it as the truth and a lie is printed in their minds. A picture of 'what a gay person supposedly is' remains with them, often into adulthood.

I read an excellent book called *Manhood* recently, written by Steve Biddulph. The book has nothing to do with homosexuality, but he does touch on it twice, very briefly. The following excerpt highlights why male homosexuality is such a big issue for all males.

> Boys feel a strong need to prove their 'masculinity'. Most parents will notice how their son drops his voice an octave when his friends are around—or refuses to kiss his baby sister goodnight if a mate is visiting.

Into this scheme of things, especially as puberty arrives, comes a strange twist. The existence of homosexuality as a biological fact in the human race, combined with many people's inability to simply be comfortable with this variation in type, means that the dread of being thought to be gay hangs over the head of any boy who is different in any way from the norm. The risk is great—and varies from being consequently rejected, ridiculed, beaten or even killed, depending on the severity of the culture. Our non-acceptance of gays actually exacts a severe price on every straight young man. It leads to the self-censoring of any kind of warmth, creativity, affection or emotionality amongst the whole male gender. 'If I'm not "macho", then I might be seen to be gay.' (In the movie *Mr Mom*, the man stayed home for a time to mind his children. He wore a hard hat all day and kept a chainsaw ticking over by the door just in case a man dropped in!)

When we oppress gay people, we oppress ourselves as well. No-one feels free to be himself or herself.

*Manhood* is one of the best books I've read in years and I highly recommend it to all Australian men, particularly young fathers. It explores many men's issues and proposes positive changes. I'm sure women would get some interesting insight into men's problems too.

There are many gay and lesbian people who have suicided because they couldn't cope, but there are far more gays and lesbians who have learned to cope with the hand they have been dealt. It is true, however, that at one time or another many of us have at least contemplated suicide. I seriously contemplated suicide about nine years ago. It was after years of trying off and on to go straight.

The root of my problems stemmed from religious indoctrination; for others it can be a completely different set of problems. I was fighting with what I felt in my heart, which conflicted with what I had been taught. One friend used to say to me, 'What is it this week, Bryce, gay or God?'

To cut a long story short, it came to the crunch when I prayed and said, 'Dear Lord, I am going to jump off this balcony trying to fight with myself and force an attraction which does not come naturally. Alternatively, I can accept my same-sex attraction and try to live the best life I can accordingly.' My belief in God was very strong, and although it still is, it has changed very much from what I was brought up to believe. I felt sure He wanted me to live, hence I didn't jump off the balcony. I requested He take away my life if I was in fact doing the wrong thing. I meant it seriously then, and I still do. I sort of put the ball back in His court. I've never had a major problem with it since that point, however I suffered a lot of unnecessary hurt getting there.

I've always loved life, but I find I love and enjoy it more the older I am. I can't believe I once contemplated taking it away. I'm so glad I had friends to help me through that rough patch, otherwise I might not be here today to talk about it. I don't want to die, even though it is inevitable. I would love to live forever. Who knows what's in store after death? I just hope it's as good as life as I know it on Earth.

I'm confident that suicide for gays and lesbians will be less of a problem, if in the future more love, tolerance and understanding are shown.

Homosexuals are often assumed to be sexually perverse. Sexual perverseness is a feature of some human behaviour, and is not a quality that is inherent in gays' and lesbians' psychological make-up. The media, however, often seem to suggest that the gay community is the wellspring of all such behaviour.

It is true that in many public toilets in many countries of the world, there are men looking to make contact with other men, either by leaving notes on the wall, playing with themselves at the urinal, or looking through peepholes.

It is illegal to have sex in a public place in Australia, but men do it regardless. Surprisingly, they are often not gay men, or at least they do not consider themselves to be. Studies carried out by the AIDS Council of New South Wales found that approximately 50 per cent of men found to be frequenting toilets did not identify themselves as being homosexual or bisexual. Even when caught in the act, they still said they were straight, and many were married men.

Others are young guys who do not know how and where to

meet other men. They might be too young or too embarrassed to go into a gay bar. It might be too confrontational for them and the fact that they could be seen could be frightening. They may not know that gay bars exist. Meeting someone in a toilet might seem anonymous and non-confronting.

I believe that the continuance of this behaviour is related to the stigma which is still associated with homosexuality. Along with this stigma comes disgust, embarrassment and in some cases self-hate. Many men and women cannot and will never accept that they are attracted to their own sex. They deny their feelings and try to suppress their attraction. It might be like trying to say, 'OK, I'm not going to eat.' It gets harder and harder to say no, and eventually the desire becomes overwhelming.

There could easily be tens of thousands of men and women living closeted lives in Australia and New Zealand because of fear. Gays and lesbians are accused of crying discrimination, but it is true that there is still dreadful discrimination towards gays and lesbians in some areas of our society.

Many men and women cannot tell the truth for fear of losing everything. Honesty might mean losing a husband or wife, losing the love of children, losing respect in the workplace, losing stature in the community and losing friends and family.

The sexual urge and the desire to eat are well renowned as being the strongest driving forces in human nature. If sexual urges are not dealt with and satisfied they can become all consuming. Luckily, there is no shortage of places in the big cities for gays and lesbians to mix and meet one another openly and naturally. Even in many country areas there are gay and lesbian groups where friendships might begin.

Many people mistakenly tend to link homosexuality and paedophilia together. Media attention has highlighted recent cases of adult men molesting young boys, however statistics show that adult men are far more likely to molest young girls.

The following information is taken from a paper written by Adam M. Tomison and published by the Australian Institute of Family Studies, entitled 'Issues in Child Abuse Prevention':

> Sexual abuse has been documented as occurring on children of
> all ages and both sexes, and is committed predominantly by

men, who are commonly members of the child's family, family friends or other trusted adults in positions of authority . . .

Statistics from the Australian Institute of Health and Welfare report, 'Child Abuse and Neglect, Australia 1994–95' (AGPS Canberra, 1996) show 30 615 substantiated cases of child abuse and neglect, 16 per cent of these cases were sexual abuse. Females were victims in 76 per cent of these cases.

Tomison sums up,

> Overall, what little evidence there is, although flawed, appears to indicate that sexual orientation does not play a part in child sexual assault typologies, and that the assumption that paedophiles who engage in same-sex sexual abuse are homosexuals is more a societal myth than a reality.

Child abuse is something we must do everything we can to stamp out. Hopefully, continuing studies will highlight further how we can deal with this serious problem.

Some parents think, Who converted my son or daughter? With regard to this, I would like to explain my situation in greater detail.

Even before I started school I remember being attracted to another kid. I must have been three or four years of age. It certainly was not a sexual feeling, because I did not know what a sexual feeling was. I liked being with him, and I enjoyed going around to his house to play. We would climb trees together, have morning tea on our own special little table and just enjoy each other's company.

But I remember wanting to show affection to him, even at that early age. Why I wanted to be affectionate, I don't know. Maybe all kids are like that. I guessed it would be a nice feeling to have a cuddle—like giving my cat a cuddle, a pat or letting it sleep on my bed. I knew it would feel good. It was a very innocent feeling. Nothing ever happened with that boy.

Then in kindergarten, at age five, I remember being really keen on this girl called Sindy. She was such a cutie. I think my dad has kept some of the poems and tape recordings of me talking about her. I was infatuated by her beauty. She had beautiful blond curly hair, an olive complexion and bright blue eyes that were always sparkling. It brings a smile to my face to think about Sindy. Dad says I swore that one day I would marry her.

Although I was keen on Sindy, there were the other feelings brewing that I knew weren't talked about. They were for my mates. I did not know they were wrong. All I knew was that nobody else talked about such feelings. How was I to know I was different? I assumed I was like everyone else.

The things my parents told me not to do I pretty much didn't do. They told me not to be 'dirty' with little girls and I wasn't. To me, even at five years of age, it didn't seem unnatural to play around with other boys. Lots of little boys used to do it and I'm sure they still do. And to be more specific, I'm talking about playing with each other's penises.

Incidentally, boys playing with one another in childhood appears to have no influence on adulthood sexuality. A high proportion of men, if able to be honest on the subject, would admit to having fooled around with other boys when they were that age.

Over the years several people have asked me, 'Why do men turn gay?' I never turned gay. I grew up that way. Sure, it was not obvious to those around me that I was growing up any differently, because in fact I was not. I simply had a same-sex attraction. Everything else about me was and still is the same. It's like asking, 'Why did you grow up heterosexual?' It just happens.

The development of the differences that make us all individuals may be attributable to certain experiences, but they can be difficult to pinpoint. Many of our personality traits, likes and dislikes develop through a combination of experiences. What is passed on through our genes clearly has much influence in our development, but does not dictate everything we are.

I developed a same-sex attraction. For what reason, I do not know and it does not matter. I knew that I was meant to do 'the done thing', get married and have kids, so I naturally planned to do it just like everyone else.

Once I had reached puberty I realised my attraction towards the same sex was getting stronger. As sex issues started to be talked about through high school I realised that my feelings really were quite different from what was being explained and what was being talked about. I knew there must be other people who felt like me, because I had had experiences from time to time with other boys. But I had no one with whom I could talk these issues over.

The concept that I was recruited by another homosexual is not applicable to me. My homosexuality is certainly not something that was caused by some other person. It just happened. I am certain there is a cause, but I am also certain it was caused by hundreds of different things—some of these things I believe are inborn.

There may be instances where people are influenced by others, but generally I doubt this is the case. If a heterosexual man or woman was encouraged or even forced to have sex with another of the same sex, surely they wouldn't do it again unless there was already a relatively strong feeling of same-sex attraction?

Many straight people think they know definitively what a gay person looks, sounds and acts like. Some still believe that gay men are all effeminate and weak; that they lisp, wear lots of pink and bright colours, leer and lust after all other men.

Lesbians are often assumed to be man-haters who dress like men and prey upon young girls. Rough, tough, strong and macho, they hate everything and everybody.

These personality traits may be applicable in varying degrees to some homosexuals, but certainly not all. Most gay people look, act, sound and behave no differently from anyone else you might bump into on a street, sit next to on a train or work alongside in your job. The invisibility of gays and lesbians is the reason why many people can't grasp the possible 'one-in-ten' incidence of homosexuality in our community that is often talked about.

Misinformation about homosexuals has been portrayed in movies and the media over the years. Mardi Gras, for example, is probably the only exposure many Australians have to homosexuality, so naturally some assume all gays to be like those they see in the Mardi Gras. Gays that look like anyone you might bump into on a street are not newsworthy.

Incidentally, don't believe that homosexuals have 'Gaydar' for identifying who is and isn't gay or lesbian. It's like trying to guess who does and doesn't like chocolate. We do not know what is going through other people's heads, particularly if they choose not to disclose it or even to hide it.

If you wonder why some gays and lesbians do behave differently from 'the norm', consider what being gay or lesbian might have been like 30 years ago. Same-sex relations were illegal in most parts of the world and homosexuality was listed as a psychological disorder.

Persecution by society forced many homosexuals to live two lives—the one where they fitted in to everyday life and appeared to be 'normal' and then their secret life, which was often only known to other homosexuals. This subculture still exists, however it is blending in and becoming more a part of mainstream life every day.

A group of people brought together by a common cause often develop unspoken codes and ethics. Many groups can potentially be recognised by dress, speech and behaviour. Look at religious groups, sporting groups, theatre lovers or country folk. I guess homosexuals similarly adopted unique behaviours which may have become exaggerated further because gay and lesbian people needed ways to identify each other.

Recognising that gay and lesbian people may have needed to behave and act a little differently in the past just to survive might help some of us to be a little less judgemental now. Young people who are gay or lesbian and need role models will obviously affect mannerisms of the older people they look up to. So even though it may not be necessary to act any differently today, it is only natural that characteristics of a previous generation will be carried on.

As gay and lesbian people continue to come out and be honest with friends, family and workmates, there will be less of a need for separateness and different behaviour. This is clearly happening.

Increasing numbers of young gays and lesbians are finding today that they do not need to hide their sexuality from their family and friends. The need to become part of a separate community is not as crucially important for as many because they are finding more acceptance at home with the family and friends they grew up with. There is still a long way to go, though.

I find it strange that we can look at some supposedly normal attitudes that are so destructive. For example, there are movies that show violence, and we don't even think twice about the effect they might have on the minds of ourselves or our children. We have tens of thousands of people in the world dying every day from starvation, and many of us don't pay it a second thought. Pollution, destruction of our rainforests and war are having a huge impact on our whole environment, but too little is happening too slowly to reverse the damage. Such things can be overlooked and even considered normal. Yet two consenting adults of the same sex who love each other are considered by some to be 'not normal'. I'm sorry if the picture of my partner John and I in bed together is not attractive. I don't try and picture a straight couple in bed together and the intricacies of what gives them their sexual gratification. I wonder why people are so fascinated with what I supposedly do and don't do. If it's between consenting adults, who's business is it but their own? All my partner and I usually do is hug, followed by a night of snoring!

I hope I have clarified a few of the misconceptions surrounding homosexuality. I hope this book will lead you on to further thoughts and exploration. There is plenty of help out there if you seek it.

*My Child is Gay* was never intended to be authoritative. There are plenty of excellent books available for parents. A good range is available in Australia through The Bookshop in Sydney or Hares & Hyenas in Melbourne. Outside Australia, I suggest you order on the Internet through Amazon or Barnes & Noble.

There is a list of support groups for parents and helplines for gays and lesbians on pp. 187–9.

The hardest thing I struck in compiling this book was instilling confidence in parents to share their story to help others. When time permits, I hope to follow up *My Child is Gay* with a more comprehensive book of a similar style, maybe including stories from children, family, friends and healthcare workers as well as parents. If you might be interested in participating, please photocopy the More Information page and forward it to me. I will keep you informed of any developments.

I hope this book was helpful. I wish you every success in everything you do. Remember—talk about it.

# APRIL FOOL'S DAY

Following is an excerpt from Bryce Courtenay's *April Fool's Day*. This book should be a 'must' read for all parents. It is the true story of the life of Damon Courtenay, Bryce Courtenay's son, who died with AIDS just a few years ago. Damon was not gay—he contracted the disease through a blood transfusion. In his life and the lives of his family, there was to be a fair amount of contact with homosexuality.

There are a few reasons I have included this rather extended and sad excerpt. Whilst compiling *My Child is Gay*, I have discovered a prevalent notion that homosexuality does not need to be talked about. Some people wish that gays and lesbians would just keep quiet, maybe because questions surrounding sexuality are confronting and embarrassing for them and do not fit in with what they have been taught. Some people might prefer not to talk about it at all and push it under the carpet.

Others might feel that homosexuality does not need to be talked about because it is no longer an issue. They might be unaware that homophobia is still alive and kicking in some people's minds.

These attitudes do not help the parent who is confronted with news that their child is gay or lesbian. It is easy to be critical of the parents in this excerpt who reacted in this manner, but they are a product of a society which has been brought up to think this way.

Heart-breaking stories like this motivated me to compile *My Child is Gay*. This excerpt painfully reinforces the need to make available more information and support to parents. I am especially impressed by Bryce Courtenay's attitude towards John. John's sexuality is not an issue for Bryce, and although I guess it's easier when it's someone else's son, his response is one to be admired.

Towards the end of Damon's first stay at Marks Pavilion an incident occurred which shocked and saddened him tremendously and might have been one of the causes of the deep malaise or depression he was to fall into not long after leaving hospital. In the room next door to his own was a young man called John (in most cases only first names are used in AIDS wards) who was also suffering from AIDS-related pneumonia. His entry into hospital had been delayed and he'd had a tremendous fight on his hands, but now seemed to be over the worst.

But, while he'd been in hospital nobody had visited him. Rick [the nurse] explained to Damon that John was in the navy and his friends were not in Sydney and that his parents lived in the country. Damon, who by this time was sufficiently well to be allowed out of bed for two or three hours every day, spent a lot of his time just sitting with John, who seemed to be making a very slow recovery and wasn't yet off the danger list. Damon has always been a sharing person and soon we were bringing what we could for John, when we visited Damon, which was precious little as he was still very ill.

Benita [Bryce's wife] would visit Damon every morning and Celeste [Damon's girlfriend] would go straight from university so that she saw him every afternoon, while I would leave work at about seven and take the evening shift. One evening, Damon confided in me that he'd sometimes wake up at night to hear John sobbing and delirious, shouting, 'Mum and Dad please forgive me!' Damon explained that it was like hearing a terribly distraught little boy, first the sobs and then his plaintive wail to be forgiven.

'He says it over and over again, Dad, like he's heartbroken but doesn't know what he's done. We have to do something, nobody has visited him since he came in.' I suggested that Damon try to find out where John's parents lived and, if it was a question of money we could help, maybe fly them up or down to Sydney and put them up in a hotel for a couple of nights.

Damon went to work, but without success; John shook his head, too ill or weak or simply not wanting to reply. Rick confided in Damon that John's prognosis wasn't good. 'He doesn't have anything to live for; when this happens they often just give up,' he observed.

Then one day John had a visitor, a young woman who was the sister of a shipmate and had received a letter from her brother on HMAS *Perth* asking her to visit John. She hadn't known John previously and of course she was shocked by what she saw. Their conversation was awkward, she was young and shy and quite unprepared for anything like this, so she didn't stay very long but promised to come back if she could get away from work again.

Damon, seeing that she was about to depart, left his bed and waited at the front desk of the hospital until she arrived; confronting her, he asked if she knew where John's parents lived. She didn't seem too sure. 'In Blacktown or Bankstown, one of them. I know because my brother once told me, but I don't know which one now,' she shrugged. 'I can't remember nothing more.'

That night Rick went home and got on the phone and called everyone in the book by the name of Baker and who was located in or near either suburb. Baker is a pretty common surname and after about four hours he finally located a family who had a son called John who was in the Australian navy and on HMAS *Perth*.

Bingo!

Rick explained to Damon that they had somehow to get John's permission to make the call to his family. 'He's very ill and we can't just have his parents drop in on him,' he explained.

'But why?' Damon asked. 'Surely they'd want to see him, come what may?'

Rick explained that gay people often lived a life of which parents were oblivious and that John's guilt could be terrible. 'Just because you're gay doesn't mean that you're not influenced by all the values your parents hold. The church, what friends would think, the relations, all that working-class crap. John's in the navy, his dad's probably proud as punch and thinks he's practically the captain by now, a real son of a gun!'

Damon went to work on John, but again this was to no avail and that night, when I visited, Damon was exhausted himself, needing more oxygen than usual. Quietly, between bouts with the oxygen mask, he explained what had happened. 'Dad, Rick says John's getting worse and may not make it and he'll die without seeing his Mum and Dad or even having them give him a hug or saying goodbye!' Tears were running down Damon's cheeks. 'It's not fair, he didn't do anything wrong!'

I held Damon's hand, feeling helpless, saying nothing, unable to think of anything to say. In the next room, we could hear the hissing sound of John's breathing apparatus and his heart monitor and, above it all, his laboured breath. 'Dad, will you talk to him?' Damon asked finally.

I rose and walked the few feet through the connecting door, feeling a little panic-stricken and I am ashamed to say a bit foolish. John's room was in semi-darkness with only the small night light above his bed. His breathing was laboured and his chest was rising and falling as though each inward breath brought him pain. The room smelt of the peaches Benita had brought the previous day, which were in a paper bag on his bedside console, three hothouse peaches, a blush of pink on the downy skin, one halfway out of the brown paper packet. They'd been brought in the hope that they might tempt him to eat something. Now I noted that they remained in the half-open bag untouched.

I sat down beside John and took his hand. It was a surprisingly big hand even for a big lad. It was cool and slightly clammy to the touch, a hand that could have come from generations of people who'd worked hard for a living. A big, practical hand, I thought, probably like his father's. John's hand lay limp in my own and I had no idea whether he was fully conscious as his eyes remained closed as I entered the room and sat beside his bed. I cleared my throat. 'Good evening, John.' I paused for a second then continued, 'John, if you can hear me just nod your head, just a little from side to side or, if you like, squeeze my hand. Don't try to talk, just a squeeze or nod of your head.'

In the semi-darkness I thought I saw his head nod, almost imperceptibly, although his hand remained limp in my own.

'John, please let me call your parents,' I said gently. 'No matter what's happened between you, as a parent of three sons I know they'd want to be with you now.' I waited a few moments then added, 'John, if you agree just squeeze my hand. Just a tiny squeeze.'

I waited but his hand remained limp, inert in my own. 'Please, just a tiny squeeze, or if you like, just nod your head again.' But still there wasn't any life in his hand and no movement of his head. Finally, after sitting with John for a little while longer, I returned to Damon's room. I was disappointed but didn't know what else I could do, though I must confess I was pretty certain John had heard me and that I had failed.

At ten the following morning Damon called me at work from hospital, he was terribly excited. 'Dad, John told Rick this morning it was OK, to call his parents!' Damon started to cough over the phone, the excitement too much for him. 'They're coming this afternoon, his parents are coming this afternoon to see him,' he gasped then added in a thin, chesty voice, 'he's going to be all right, you'll see, he'll get better now!'

I arrived to see Damon that evening to find him in a great deal of distress.

'You came too late, Dad,' he sobbed. For several minutes I could get nothing from him, just the same phrase, 'You came too late!' Finally he managed to tell me what had happened.

John's parents had arrived late in the afternoon. 'They were, you know, just ordinary working-class people like everybody else. Rick met them as they came in and John's father wanted to know what the matter was, you know, why was his son so sick? Rick took them to the TV lounge and asked them to take a seat. John's mum sat down but his father remained standing. John's mum had not spoken a word since they'd entered the hospital, she'd just followed them to the TV lounge. Rick said she looked scared. Rick then explained to John's father that he was very ill, that John had a kind of special pneumonia.'

'Why wasn't we told before?' John's father demanded to know.

'Well, I told you on the phone this morning,' Rick replied.

'No, before. Why wasn't we told before?'

Rick cleared his throat. 'We couldn't get your phone number

until I phoned two days ago; it was just a punt,' he explained, then added, 'I'd already phoned dozens and dozens of numbers, maybe fifty Bakers until I got you.'

'Why didn't you tell me then, on the bloody phone! You just asked those questions about the navy and his ship and hung up. We thought he'd deserted, jumped ship or somethin' real bad like that!'

'I'm sorry, Mr Baker.' Rick smiled, trying to disarm the big man who towered above him. 'You see we were very worried, John is very sick and we knew only that you lived somewhere in Bankstown or Blacktown but that's all. He was too sick to tell us how to contact you. I couldn't tell you before I had his permission to call you. I mean, we didn't know if you . . . you,' Rick hesitated, clearing his throat, 'know, knew about John?'

John's dad looked down at Rick, he was a tough-looking guy, big and rough, the sort of man you made a mental note not to annoy in the pub, and he was very angry. 'Knew what? Knew bloody what!'

Rick looked at Mrs Baker for help, but she was seated with her hands in her lap not looking up. He talked directly to her, not looking at John's old man standing beside him. 'Mrs Baker, your son has AIDS, he's very sick with a sort of pneumonia called PCP, he wants to see you.' The woman gasped and looked up at her husband, clutching at her neck with both hands. John's dad looked at his wife. 'You hear that, woman?' It was as though he was accusing her of something, blaming her for his son's predicament.

Damon was weeping again. 'Dad they went in and stayed perhaps for twenty minutes. John's mum sat on one side of the room and his dad on the other as far away from him as they could get. They didn't touch him, they didn't even speak to him. John's mum just sat and looked into her hands. Maybe she was crying, I couldn't see from the way she held her head.

'I couldn't see his dad at all, I just knew where the chair was he was sitting on, it was about four feet from John's bed. All I could hear was John crying and him saying, "Forgive me, Mum and Dad, *please* forgive me!" Just like at night. He was begging them. His voice was terribly laboured and I knew how hard it was for him to speak. He'd get it out and then lie panting and then get the oxygen mask up and he'd try to get enough air to say it again. He kept repeating it, over and over, begging his mum and dad to forgive him, until I thought he was going to die; but his parents didn't move, didn't say anything! His mum didn't even look up.'

Damon stopped, too upset to continue. I was shocked myself and close to tears. 'It's hard, darling. It's very hard for a man and woman like that to be confronted suddenly with something like this. Perhaps they don't know how sick John is. Rick says that, often, when people hear of their son's homosexuality and AIDS condition together for the first time their reaction is traumatic, just like John's parents today; but then they go home and think it out and come back the next day and they are soon reconciled. People like that just don't understand, they've been conditioned, often since childhood, to think homosexuality is a sin or a terrible disgrace.'

Damon wiped his eyes and I wasn't sure he'd been listening to me because he continued, anxious to get his story over. 'Then I heard John's dad say, "Come, woman!" and John's mum got up and they walked out. They didn't even stop at the door to say goodbye.'

Damon was howling again and I cradled him and rocked him and tried to comfort him. It was only then that I realised that John's breathing apparatus wasn't making its customary hissing noise and that the door to his adjoining room, which was usually open, was now shut.

'Is John all right?' I asked.

Damon stopped sniffing and looked up at me. 'He's dead. He died an hour ago!'

The remainder of the story came out later. Immediately his parents had departed, Damon and Rick had gone in to see John in an attempt to comfort him. John hadn't said anything, he just lay exhausted, his breath coming in great heaves from behind the oxygen mask. Tears just kept running down his dark stubbled cheeks, running along the edge of the oval oxygen mask on to his chin and down the front of his neck and into the V-top of his pyjama jacket. Big, silent tears that just seemed to squeeze out every couple of seconds.

Rick pulled up a chair and Damon did the same and they

sat on either side of the bed and held one large hand each. There wasn't anything they could say, they just held John's hands. Finally Rick had to go because they were paging him to an urgent call and Damon was left alone with John.

After a while John seemed to be wanting to get his oxygen mask off but he couldn't seem to raise his free hand, getting it as far as his chest before it fell back to his side again. Damon leaned over and removed it and John lay panting, gasping for breath. 'They . . . they . . . wouldn't even touch me!' A great moan rose up from his inside and then he started to cough and sort of choke and Damon held the oxygen mask over his mouth so he could breathe again.

Damon turned to me. 'Dad, I told him that you'd be coming tonight, that you'd hug him, that you'd be his dad as much as he wanted.' Damon looked up at me, his eyes swollen from crying. Suddenly he buried his head into my chest. 'But you got here too late,' he sobbed.

# FURTHER INFORMATION

## Parents, Families and Friends of Lesbians and Gays (PFLAG)

PFLAG is run primarily by parents offering support to other parents. PFLAG groups or contacts exist in many towns and cities in Australia. They offer telephone support, have helpful literature and can recommend suitable books. Many have regular meetings where parents can meet up with one another. It is best to call the PFLAG number listed for your state to get contact numbers in your local area.

**Australia**

| | |
|---|---|
| New South Wales | (02) 9294 1002 |
| Victoria | (03) 9827 8408 |
| Queensland | 0400 767 832 |
| Western Australia | (08) 9228 1005 |
| South Australia (PSP Flag) | (08) 8369 0718 |
| Tasmania | (03) 6234 2372 |
| Australian Capital Territory | (02) 6251 1599 |

**New Zealand**  (03) 466 4600

**USA**

There are several hundred PFLAG support groups in North America. To contact your local group check with the PFLAG head office.

PFLAG Head Office USA
1726 M Street NW, Suite 400
Washington DC 20036
Tel: 202 467 8180
Web: www.pflag.org

## Other organisations

The following organisations offer counselling and/or referrals to the appropriate support groups for gays, lesbians and their families in Australia and New Zealand.

### New South Wales

Gay and Lesbian Counselling Service of NSW
(02) 8594 9596 or 1800 184 527 (freecall in NSW/ACT outside Sydney)

### Victoria

Gay and Lesbian Switchboard Victoria
(03) 9827 8544 or 1800 184 527 (freecall in Vic outside Melbourne)

### Queensland

Queensland AIDS Council
1800 155 141 (freecall in Qld)

### Western Australia

Gay and Lesbian Community Services
(08) 9420 7201 or 1800 184 527 (freecall in WA outside Perth)

### South Australia

Gay and Lesbian Community Services
(08) 8422 8400 or 1800 182 233 (freecall in SA outside Adelaide)

### Tasmania

Gay and Lesbian Switchboard Victoria
1800 184 527 (freecall in Tas)

### Australian Capital Territory

Telephone Help, Referral and Outreach Bureau
(02) 6247 2726 or
GLCS
1800 184 527

## Northern Territory

Northern Territory AIDS and Hepatitis Council
(08) 8941 1711 or 1800 880 899 (freecall in NT outside Darwin)

## Books

Recommended bookshops are listed below. They offer mail order.

### The Bookshop Darlinghurst
207 Oxford Street
Darlinghurst  NSW  2010
Australia
Tel: (02) 9331 1103
Web: www.thebookshop.com.au

### Hares & Hyenas
135 Commercial Road
South Yarra Vic  3141
Tel: (03) 9824 0110
Web: www.hares-hyenas.com.au

If you are outside Australia and have internet access, **Amazon** may be a good option. You can search for books under 'Parents of Gays'. Alternatively, search for *My Child is Gay* and you will find links to other suitable titles. Amazon can be found at www.amazon.com

## More information

If you think you might be interested in contributing your story to a future edition of *My Child is Gay* please let me know. If you have other feedback you can contact me on the address below.

Bryce McDougall
PO Box 1020
Potts Point  NSW  1335
Australia
Email: bryce@unwired.com.au